P9-BZK-680

Incentives for Faculty Vitality

Roger G. Baldwin, *Editor*

NEW DIRECTIONS FOR HIGHER EDUCATION
MARTIN KRAMER, *Editor-in-Chief*

Number 51, September 1985

Paperback sourcebooks in
The Jossey-Bass Higher Education Series

Jossey-Bass Inc., Publishers
San Francisco • London

Roger G. Baldwin (Ed.).
Incentives for Faculty Vitality.
New Directions for Higher Education, no. 51.
Volume XIII, no. 3.
San Francisco: Jossey-Bass, 1985.

New Directions for Higher Education
Martin Kramer, *Editor-in-Chief*

New Directions for Higher Education, is published quarterly by Jossey-
Bass Inc., Publishers (publication number USPS 990-880). *New Directions*
is numbered sequentially—please order extra copies by sequential
number. The volume and issue numbers above are included for the
convenience of libraries. Second-class postage rates paid at San Francisco,
California, and at additional mailing offices.

Correspondence:
Subscriptions, single-issue orders, change of address notices, undelivered
copies, and other correspondence should be sent to Subscriptions,
Jossey-Bass Inc., Publishers, 433 California Street, San Francisco,
California 94104.

Editorial correspondence should be sent to
Martin Kramer, 2807 Shasta Road, Berkeley, California 94708.

Library of Congress Catalog Card Number 85-60830

International Standard Serial Number ISSN 0271-0560

International Standard Book Number ISBN 87589-749-5

Cover art by WILLI BAUM

Manufactured in the United States of America

Ordering Information

The paperback sourcebooks listed below are published quarterly and can be ordered either by subscription or single-copy.

Subscriptions cost $40.00 per year for institutions, agencies, and libraries. Individuals can subscribe at the special rate of $30.00 per year *if payment is by personal check.* (Note that the full rate of $40.00 applies if payment is by institutional check, even if the subscription is designated for an individual.) Standing orders are accepted.

Single copies are available at $9.95 when payment accompanies order, and *all single-copy orders under $25.00 must include payment.* (California, New Jersey, New York, and Washington, D.C., residents please include appropriate sales tax.) For billed orders, cost per copy is $9.95 plus postage and handling. (Prices subject to change without notice.)

Bulk orders (ten or more copies) of any individual sourcebook are available at the following discounted prices: 10–49 copies, $8.95 each; 50–100 copies, $7.96 each; over 100 copies, *inquire.* Sales tax and postage and handling charges apply as for single copy orders.

To ensure correct and prompt delivery, all orders must give either the *name of an individual* or an *official purchase order number.* Please submit your order as follows:

Subscriptions: specify series and year subscription is to begin.
Single Copies: specify sourcebook code (such as, HE1) and first two words of title.

Mail orders for United States and Possessions, Latin America, Canada, Japan, Australia, and New Zealand to:
Jossey-Bass Inc., Publishers
433 California Street
San Francisco, California 94104

Mail orders for all other parts of the world to:
Jossey-Bass Limited
28 Banner Street
London EC1Y 8QE

New Directions for Higher Education Series
Martin Kramer, *Editor-in-Chief*

HE1 *Facilitating Faculty Development,* Mervin Freedman
HE2 *Strategies for Budgeting,* George Kaludis
HE3 *Services for Students,* Joseph Katz
HE4 *Evaluating Learning and Teaching,* C. Robert Pace
HE5 *Encountering the Unionized University,* Jack H. Schuster
HE6 *Implementing Field Experience Education,* John Duley

Contents

Editor's Notes

This source book examines the range of incentives higher education institutions can employ to support faculty vitality. Converging forces in society have focused attention on the vitality of the academic profession. Growing interest in the morale, achievements, and effectiveness of college professors—in other words, faculty vitality—is part of a larger national concern about productivity, quality, and the ability to keep pace with foreign competitors. A concurrent trend is an increasing concern with the conditions of work life, meaningful career development, and the relationship between organizational cultures and worker performance. Phenomenally popular books, such as *In Search of Excellence, Megatrends,* and *The Change Masters,* illustrate a national concern for renewal and excellence. These books demonstrate a desire to be all we can be as individuals, as organizations, and as a nation.

As one of the most influential sectors of our society, higher education and the people who staff it have come under scrutiny. Several recent national reports have suggested that colleges and universities could be performing considerably better than they are. These reports attribute much of the responsibility for higher education's problems to the dominant values and structure of the academic profession. Evidence suggests that in many institutions professors have not kept pace with the current information explosion or responded satisfactorily to the changing educational needs of a pluralistic, technologically oriented society.

Higher education institutions recognize that their quality depends on the vitality of the academics they employ. Hence, colleges and universities are searching for effective ways to keep professors up-to-date in their fields and actively engaged in their multiple roles as teachers and scholars. The basic goal of institutions is to capitalize on the strengths and maximize the effectiveness of each individual faculty member. This objective requires an organizational climate that stimulates professors to do their best work. It calls for incentives that encourage faculty members to grow professionally, to be innovative and flexible, and to invest themselves heavily in their careers.

This source book studies the issue of incentives to enhance faculty vitality from several useful perspectives. The chapters discuss the psychological and sociological foundations of effective incentives. More importantly, perhaps, they discuss incentives from the practical perspective of what works, what does not work, and why.

1

In the volume's introductory chapter, Baldwin and Krotseng review conditions in higher education that make incentives for faculty vitality a timely concern. They examine variables that influence professors' motivation and performance, and they conclude that a diverse range of incentives is needed to maintain the vitality of a heterogeneous professoriate. The chapter provides a brief overview of incentives used in complex organizations, particularly those incentives employed successfully by some of America's most progressive corporations.

Schuster, in Chapter Two, employs recent field research on the professoriate to identify conditions critical to faculty vitality. The chapter offers a straightforward and thought-provoking faculty vitality equation. The formula should serve as a useful tool for examining conditions related to faculty morale and effectiveness at all types of higher education institutions.

Bowen capitalizes on his experience as a dean and academic vice-president to discuss incentives in concrete and practical terms. In Chapter Three, he distinguishes among tangible and intangible and direct and indirect incentives and illustrates the value of each. Bowen offers ten keys useful in creating and implementing incentives for faculty vitality.

In Chapter Four, Bevan considers which positions within a college or university are best suited to offer incentives to professors. He carefully outlines the special roles the dean, department chair, and director of faculty development can play in fostering the vitality of faculty members.

In Chapter Five, Lawrence urges higher education to capitalize on intrinsic incentives salient at various points in the academic career. She suggests that institutional as well as faculty well-being can be enhanced by recognizing the natural search for meaning in one's work and the inherent desire to control one's work environment. By adjusting organizational expectations to accommodate changing personal attributes and needs (thus maximizing the person-environment fit), colleges and universities can promote maximum faculty vitality.

Toombs helps to place the incentive issue in a broad perspective. In Chapter Six, he examines the professional, disciplinary, and institutional contexts that influence professors' performance and shape their careers. Toombs suggests that this is a difficult time to be in the academic profession because of the ambiguous and sometimes negative circumstances in the work environment of many faculty members. His analysis makes clear that both the vitality of the academic profession as a whole and the vitality of individual professors deserve considerable attention.

Chapter Seven is a case study chronicaling one institution's continuing effort to maintain a dynamic faculty. Hamill describes a fluid, multi-dimensional faculty development strategy that has responded to changing conditions within the College of Charleston and the wider environment of higher education. The author draws from considerable

front-line experience as assistant provost for faculty services to develop a list
of practical ideas for designing and managing faculty incentives.

Wylie and Fuller, in Chapter Eight, consider how opportunities to
collaborate with colleagues from different institutions can enhance faculty
vitality. By pooling funds and expertise, colleges and universities are
sometimes able to offer services and activities that they could not offer
individually. This chapter reviews the diverse range of cooperative
professional development projects that the Great Lakes Colleges Association
sponsors, and it offers guidelines for others wishing to promote greater inter-
institutional faculty collaboration.

Settle brings the fresh perspective of an academic outsider to the
discussion of incentives to promote faculty vitality. In Chapter Nine he
borrows ideas from *In Search of Excellence* and applies them to the higher
education work place. In the concise, action-oriented manner of a corporate
memo, Settle poses questions to academic leaders (presidents, deans,
department chairs) concerning their strategies to optimize professors'
commitment and productivity in pursuit of educational excellence.

This volume on incentives to enhance faculty vitality focuses on a
topic that will remain a concern in higher education for the foreseeable future. It will be impossible to improve the quality of education if faculty
members fall behind in their fields or become ambivalent about their work.
The authors carefully consider the conditions needed to sustain the esprit de
corps of the academic profession. The insights they present should be useful
to individual professors, institutional leaders, and government policy makers
who wish to preserve the fragile vitality that is the essence of a successful
higher education system.

Roger G. Baldwin
Editor

*Roger G. Baldwin is assistant professor of higher education at the
College of William and Mary, in Williamsburg, Virginia.*

For faculty members to perform at the highest levels of excellence requires designing and implementing an array of appropriate, effective incentives.

Incentives in the Academy: Issues and Options

Roger G. Baldwin, Marsha V. Krotseng

Most people who work in a college or university can think of professors who have been revitalized by the appropriate incentive offered at the proper time. Two brief cases illustrate this phenomenon:

1. A competent but uninspired midcareer college professor is "brought to life" by a small research grant that enables him to pursue a blossoming area of interest. The grant does much more than provide funds for travel and a research assistant. It demonstrates that the professor is a capable scholar who holds the respect of his colleagues. To the casual observer, the research award may seem like a standard academic practice. But to the floundering professor, it offers a powerful incentive that can increase his professional vitality and value to his institution.

2. A congratulatory note from the university president, including a request to chair the institution's long-range planning committee, offers a challenge and a sense of direction to an energetic, newly promoted associate professor. The letter eclipses any thoughts she has of slipping into the comfortable but uncreative routine that seduces many tenured professors.

Those who work in a college or university can also think of professors who continue on a virtual treadmill, going through the motions of academic life without enthusiasm or commitment. Finn (1984) has indicted higher education on this very count; he asserts that many professors do little more

R. G. Baldwin (Ed.). *Incentives for Faculty Vitality.* New Directions for
Higher Education, no. 51. San Francisco: Jossey-Bass, September 1985.

than meet their scheduled classes and then "give the same lectures year after year" (p. 33). One cannot help but wonder what it would take to rekindle the professional vitality of such individuals. What incentives could renew their involvement in their academic careers? Similarly, one wonders what incentives are needed to sustain the innovative, highly productive professors who are the hallmark of a quality institution of higher learning.

Faculty Incentives: A Timely Concern

By definition, an incentive is something that stimulates action or effort. The anticipation of a reward or the fear of punishment can act as an incentive. Organizations employ many types of incentives to shape their employees' behavior and to produce desired results. Incentives that stimulate professional growth and productive activity can heighten morale and contribute to the overall effectiveness of an organization.

Incentives that enhance faculty vitality are an important concern in higher education institutions. Professors comprise the heart of the academic enterprise. To paraphrase Smith (1978), a college or university is its faculty. The excellence of a higher education institution is equivalent to the excellence of its faculty. Hence, the character of a college or university depends heavily on the vigor and resourcefulness of its professors. An institution cannot offer a quality educational product without high-caliber, committed professors—a vital faculty.

The issue of incentives to support faculty vitality is not new. However, the issue is especially timely and significant at present because of several trends that threaten the morale and performance of professors on many college and university campuses.

A projected decline in enrollment is already influencing faculty staffing patterns. Institutions are hiring fewer new professors fresh from graduate training, and fewer established professors are advancing their careers by moving on to new positions at other institutions. As a result, the faculties at many colleges and universities are immobile and aging rapidly. Frye (1984), academic vice-president at the University of Michigan, laments the lowest rate of faculty turnover in thirty years, since it engenders budgetary and programmatic rigidity.

Opportunities for professional renewal seem to be following a comparably negative course. Centra (1985) cites evidence that institutional support for faculty development has decreased over the past decade. For example, both travel to professional meetings and sabbaticals have been victims of budget-cutting efforts at many institutions.

A general decline in the quality of academic work life appears to be underway. Austin and Gamson (1983) report that a "speed-up"—more work for the same pay—is occurring in many places. Professors are asked to assume heavier teaching and committee loads and to continue their research efforts with obsolete equipment, fewer support services, and meager financial resources. Austin and Gamson (1983, p. 88) conclude that the outcome is increased "role conflict, stress, and time pressure," which can negatively affect the performance of professional staff. This abbreviated litany of problems facing higher education clearly demonstrates that the fragile vitality of professors is threatened.

What Conditions Affect Faculty Vitality?

Clark and others (1985, p. 3) describe vitality as "those essential, yet intangible, positive qualities of individuals and institutions that enable purposeful production." Adapting Gardner's (1978) discussion of vitality to the academic profession, we would look for professors who are enthusiastic, curious, and regenerative. We would search for people who enjoy their work, reach out for new challenges, and are not afraid to risk failure. Vital professors are productive professionals in a quantitative sense. But their essence is perhaps better captured in qualitative terms that go beyond simple productivity. Clark and others (1985) suggest that quality and effectiveness are also important attributes of vital professors. In *Morale,* Gardner (1978, p. 73) writes that "a society concerned for its own continued vitality will be interested in the growth and fulfillment of individual human beings—the release of human potentialities." Similarly, higher education institutions that value their effectiveness need to release the full potential of their faculty resources.

Colleges and universities routinely employ some incentives in an effort to promote vitality in all dimensions of academic life. They hope incentives will stimulate good teaching, creative research, and valuable public service. They want incentives to promote continuous professional growth and innovative contributions to scholarship and program development.

A question colleges and universities continually confront, however, is, What organizational conditions most effectively foster faculty vitality? What types of incentives can higher education institutions offer to sustain high-quality faculty performance? Some discussion of the factors that motivate college professors and influence the quality of their work is needed in order to respond to these questions.

Intrinsic Factors Affecting Faculty Vitality. McKeachie (1979) cautions that faculty motivation is complex and cannot be explained by a simple materialistic view. He discounts the idea that faculty will automatically become more engaged in their work and professionally productive if higher education institutions simply increase the size or frequency of the incentives they offer. Veysey's (1965) historical research attributes the greatest source of faculty motivation to the academic work itself. He relates that during the late nineteenth and early twentieth centuries the "usual professor" found incentive primarily "in the belief that he was influencing other minds, either in the classroom, in his public investigations, or in both" (p. 335). Based on his extensive review of psychological research, McKeachie (1979) finds this observation equally true today. Professors like the association with college students and the opportunity to contribute to student development. They enjoy the intellectual interchange characteristic of academic life and also derive pleasure from the freedom and autonomy available in a faculty position. The implication of McKeachie's analysis is that the intrinsic satisfactions of the academic career have a greater relationship to faculty vitality than do extrinsic rewards.

Extrinsic Factors Affecting Faculty Vitality. It would, however, be naive to dismiss the impact of extrinsic factors on faculty motivation and activity. Extrinsic dimensions of academic work include such things as work load, working conditions, supervisory practices, career opportunity structures, and rewards (Austin and Gamson, 1983). Clark and Corcoran (1985, p. 112) suggest that colleges and universities need to be aware of the organizational attributes that "shape careers, aspirations, performance, and morale." Institutional practices regulating how faculty members are chosen, socialized, promoted, and rewarded are all likely to be related to professors' vitality.

Academic Reward System. The academic reward system has some influence on the behavior and productivity of college faculty members. Tuckman (1979) reports that monetary incentives exist for faculty to choose some activities over others. In research based on a national survey of professors in public and private universities, he found that participation in current administration brings substantial salary increments. He also found that publication results in salary increases, with incentives in most fields favoring article publication over the publication of books. In contrast, his research revealed that public service was rewarded monetarily in only 45 percent of the fields he sampled. Outstanding teaching (identified by the receipt of recognition for teaching excellence) was rewarded by only two of the twenty-two fields he studied.

No matter how intrinsically motivated a professor may be, it is difficult in today's competitive academic climate to ignore such strong messages about which academic activities reap rewards and which do not. McKeachie (1979) states that monetary rewards are not so important for what they will buy as for what they symbolize. They communicate the values of a professor's colleagues and institution. Similarly, promotion tells an academic that he or she is esteemed by peers. Other types of institutional rewards, such as special status designations, prizes, and special privileges, can also send clear signals to faculty members. It seems logical that an institution's reward structure, no matter what it emphasizes, can be a significant force in shaping the direction and intensity of professors' activities.

Conditions of Work Life. The conditions of academic work life also correlate with the motivation and performance of faculty members. History corroborates this point as shown in Veysey's (1965) discussion of the capabilities and personalities of various professors of a century ago. "It remained an important question," he writes (p. 432), "whether the atmosphere of American academic institutions tended over the years to promote or to anesthetize the aspirations" of the typical faculty member. In some instances "an institution clearly brought together a cluster of individuals who fertilized one another's potentials" while in other cases "academic constraints almost certainly contributed to a loss of creative power" (p. 432). Clearly, the distribution of a contemporary professor's work load (among the classroom, governance activities, and the research lab, for example) influences the amount of enthusiasm and energy he or she can devote to various academic pursuits. The way an institution structures a professor's time also affects vitality (Blackburn, 1979). A schedule that leaves two days a week free from classroo n commitments is likely to foster more scholarship than a schedule that requires daily class meetings encompassing both morning and afternoon.

Similarly, a campus's structural and physical arrangements can facilitate the effectiveness of professors. A streamlined committee system with a minimum number of meetings can protect professors' precious energy and ability to concentrate. Attractive, well-maintained facilities and state-of-the-art equipment can make academic work efficient and productive. Comfortable meeting places (for example, a faculty dining room or library lounge), where faculty members naturally converge, can facilitate the exchange of ideas, professional collaboration, and the spread of enthusiasm.

Faculty support systems can also affect professors' performance. Secretarial support, library services, and computing assistance are just a few of the support services that can facilitate academic work—or serve as a source of faculty frustration.

Less-structured elements of the academic work place are, likewise, critical to professors' growth and achievement. Vehicles for systematic exchanges of ideas and information (such as attendance at professional meetings and journal subscriptions) provide the stimulus for academics to remain current in their fields of interest. Research demonstrates that the most prolific scholars are those who are in touch with a wide variety of professionals beyond their own campuses (Finkelstein, 1982). A similar leavening function is provided by lectures, symposiums, and concert series that bring fresh ideas or models of excellence to a campus. Such activities can infuse faculty members with a sense of excitement that can carry over into their own work.

Blackburn and Baldwin (1983) further emphasize the close relationship between a campus's work environment and faculty vitality. They acknowledge that monetary compensation is an important consideration for professors, but they report that academics base "primary decisions about what college to join and what activities to perform more on the basis of the conditions of work than they do on the dollars and cents they are offered" (p. 10). Factors entering into these primary decisions include having stimulating colleagues and students, opportunities to teach favorite courses, and avenues for scholarly growth.

Elements of an Environment Conducive to Faculty Vitality. The available evidence seems to support McKeachie's previously stated conclusion: Faculty motivation is a complex phenomenon that is not easily regulated. Many factors apparently combine to create a climate conducive to faculty achievement and vitality. "Peer support, a feeling of autonomy and control over one's work, a sense of stimulation from one's students and colleagues, and an administration that encourages, rather than restricts, faculty initiative—all of these contribute to higher levels of motivation and investment on the part of faculty members" (McKeachie, 1982, p. 462). Finkelstein (1984), in his review of research on the academic profession, observes that no single variable or group of variables seems to explain much of the variance in professors' overall job performance. In sum, the academic work place provides a context (an organizational culture) that influences both the objectives and the performance of faculty members.

Kanter (1979), drawing on research in corporations, reports that opportunity for professional growth and advancement, plus a sense of personal power or influence, has an impact on workers' aspirations. The process Kanter describes seems relevant to academic institutions as well as to corporate enterprises. In order to maintain professors' energy and commitment, colleges and universities must provide conditions that give faculty members a sense of purpose and growth. To keep faculty "among the moving," Clark and Lewis (1985, p. 249) prescribe "an opportunity and power structure that opens career paths, provides developmental activities, facilitates lateral movement across fields, that involves people in goal setting, planning, and governance, and that recognizes good performance in a variety of ways."

Put simply, higher education institutions must provide many different types of incentives if they wish to create an environment conducive to high levels of energy, quality work, ongoing professional development, and overall faculty vitality. The complex array of factors that affect professors' motivation and performance suggests that one or two principal types of incentives aimed at all faculty members are unlikely to sustain the energy and effectiveness of professors working in institutions as complex as colleges and universities.

Designing Effective Incentives

Capable professors who work in a supportive environment that offers a diverse range of incentives is the generic formula for faculty vitality. Like the recipe for an elegant soufflé, however, the prescription for faculty vitality is easier to write than to bring to fruition.

We know that the more attractive a potential reward is, the more it can motivate a person to behave in a desired way (Porter and others, 1975). The key to faculty vitality is to discover the types of incentives that are most attractive to faculty members and that will most economically and effectively stimulate professors' best work. The goal, of course, requires an understanding of the range of incentives higher education institutions are capable of offering. Moreover, it requires knowledge of the circumstances that shape the value of various incentives.

The Range of Options. Effective incentives can be intangible as well as tangible. (Schuster, in Chapter Two of this volume, and Bowen, in Chapter Three, discuss tangible and intangible incentives in greater detail.) Tangible incentives often take the form of extrinsic rewards that can be given directly by the employing institution. Salary increases, promotions, more interesting assignments, fringe benefits, and status symbols are types of tangible incentives colleges and universities can employ to encourage professors' best efforts.

Intangible incentives (incentives a person cannot see or spend, for example) can also have a powerful influence on professors' performance. Approval, praise, and other forms of meaningful attention from departmental and institutional administrators may be among an organization's most powerful forms of reinforcement (Peters and Waterman, 1982). Many intangible rewards, such as feelings of competence or self-actualization resulting from a job well done, cannot be given out by a professor's institution. What a college or university can do, however, is attempt to create conditions wherein a person can experience the natural benefits of the academic profession (Porter and others, 1975). For instance, institutions that encourage close student-faculty relationships, facilitate scholarly activity, and protect faculty from excessive bureaucratic regulation can boost professors' morale, and probably their effectiveness, without directly rewarding their hard work.

Illustrations from the Corporate Sector. As noted earlier, in many respects colleges and universities resemble other complex organizations such as corporate enterprises. For example, Keller (1983) reminds us that higher education is a "people business." And it is precisely this overarching emphasis on people that distinguishes America's best-run companies from their less productive and less successful counterparts. Colleges and universities are judged ultimately by the quality of their faculty. "Yet," observes Keller, "many campuses have strangely paid relatively little attention to the quality and productivity of their people" (p. 64). A brief review of incentives employed by progressive corporations may stimulate the higher education community to consider the wide range of techniques available to foster faculty vitality.

The corporate world recognized the crucial link between attention to employees and productivity some fifty years ago in Mayo's (1933) classic research at Western Electric's Hawthorne plant. For these people a feeling of importance—of being special—made the vital difference. Throughout *In Search of Excellence,* Peters and Waterman (1982) describe the *completeness* of the "people orientation" in such corporations as IBM, Delta, and Hewlett-Packard. Kanter's work *The Change Masters* (1983) cites the people-centered environments of Honeywell and, again, Hewlett-Packard, which communicate a sense of importance to employees. Even a recent (1985) report on America's business schools prepared by the Business-Higher Education Forum emphasizes the need to include in the curriculum such "people-management" skills as interviewing, coaching, counseling, negotiating, and motivating.

In studying exemplary companies, Peters and Waterman (1982) found not only rich systems of tangible and monetary incentives but a wide variety of nonmonetary incentives and experimental programs as well. Such rewards convey a powerful message to employees about the kind of organization the management wishes to maintain and, by extension, about appropriate employee behaviors and attitudes (Beer and others, 1985a).

Tangible incentives are most commonly thought of in monetary terms. Many industries facing declining productivity (and, increasingly, public school systems warned of the impending "rising tide of mediocrity") have implemented merit-pay systems. Although the specifics may differ from company to company, merit-pay systems are designed to motivate employees by directly relating periodic pay increases to exceptional job performance.

At Hewlett-Packard, compensation propels the constant search for innovative products and services. Project leaders are encouraged to engage in entrepreneurial behavior through significant rewards tied to successful outcomes (MacMillan and Schuler, 1985). TRW also uses compensation practices to foster innovation. Lincoln Electric has utilized both individual and group pay incentives to create a highly motivated—and a highly efficient—work force. The success of Nucor Corporation's sales efforts derives from a compensation system utilizing four different group-level incentive plans (MacMillan and Schuler, 1985).

However, as Marcaccio (1985, p. 45) observes, "Successful incentive programs must actually create incentive." Unfortunately, management's excitement over a newly proposed or established incentive program may obscure the meaning of this seemingly obvious statement. Merit pay, for example, does have limitations. It is most appropriate for those jobs in which employee performance can be readily assessed on the basis of specific criteria and then translated into a dollar amount. And, to continue functioning as a true incentive, merit pay cannot be viewed as a regularly anticipated salary increase. Nevertheless, a perception of merit pay as an across-the-board salary increase seems to be the norm: In a 1979 survey, over one half of the participating companies gave merit increases to at least 95 percent of their employees (Printz and Waldman, 1985). This raises the troublesome question of how to reward truly exceptional performance.

Printz and Waldman (1985) speculate that in future years corporate employees will earn annual merit bonuses in the form of "perk credit." American Can Company and TRW currently allow employees to apply perk credits in cafeteria-style plans. They can choose among and combine perks and wage increases. Profit sharing, flexible hours, problem counseling, physical fitness centers, and day-care facilities are among the typical perks offered. Alternative types of corporate incentives include individual bonus plans, profit-sharing plans, stock options, and early retirement plans.

Peters and Waterman (1982) describe other tangible but nonmonetary incentives employed by various firms. McDonald's, Tupperware, and IBM are among the companies offering positive reinforcements in the form of pins, buttons, badges, medals, ribbons, certificates, and trophies. McDonald's uses plaques to recognize the "crew member of the month" and annually sponsors the "All-American Hamburger Maker" contest. While on the surface such awards may appear to be contrived or insignificant, they symbolize top management's deeper concern for employees as human beings. Hence, even these seemingly trivial tokens can lift an employee's sagging spirits.

In many companies special awards honor a select few outstanding performers such as IBM's "gold circle" for the top 10 percent of its sales people. However, Rene McPherson of the Dana Corporation believes the "real key to success is helping the middle 60 percent a few steps up the ladder" (Peters and Waterman, 1982, p. 269). "When the number of awards is high, it makes the perceived possibility of winning something high as well. And then the average man will stretch to achieve" (p. 269). From this perspective, the "gold circle" may be less significant than the One Hundred Percent Club, which covers over two thirds of the IBM sales force.

Kanter (1983) suggests that such formal awards and public recognition may make less difference to the receiver than to observers who see that high objectives are attainable—and that their contributions may be similarly noticed, applauded, and remembered. Kanter also reveals that innovative companies typically " 'invested' in people before they carried out their projects" (p. 154) rather than rewarding them later for a job well done. In many cases the successful completion of one assignment led to getting the budget or assignment for an even larger task. Here, the reward "consisted largely of getting to carry out the project in the first place" (p. 154).

Lockheed Missiles and Space Company, Inc., of Sunnyvale, California, has adopted a somewhat more unusual program of incentives to reduce employee absenteeism and to combat rising health costs (Halcrow, 1985). Under the guidance of its medical department, the company initiated an overall wellness program including a carefully monitored three-month diet program ("Take It Off '83") for employees and their families. The overall response and benefits achieved have prompted Lockheed to make the program an annual event. Likewise, some of the best American and Japanese corporations have encouraged employee physical fitness by daily calisthenics. IBM, for example, provides running tracks and tennis courts.

As McKeachie's (1979) work implies, these tangible benefits, however potent, may be ineffective without reinforcement from more intangible incentives. IBM, Texas Instruments, and Kodak, as well as other consistently well-managed corporations, all inspire in their employees that vital yet intangible sense of pride or belonging. This spirit emanates from the company's basic philosophy. At Dana, for example, it is fostered by the belief that the corporation has "an obligation to provide training and the opportunity for development to . . . productive people who want to improve their skills, expand their career opportunities, or simply further their general education. [Dana seeks to] create incentive programs that rely on ideas and suggestions, as well as on hard work to establish a reward pool" (Peters and Waterman, 1982, p. 249). Hewlett-Packard's founder, Bill Hewlett, also affirms the importance of a proper environment, which includes "treating every individual with consideration and respect and recognizing personal achievements" (Peters and Waterman, 1982, p. 244).

Kanter (1983) calls this the "culture of pride"—pride in the company's achievement and in the abilities of individuals. Such phrases as the "H-P [Hewlett-Packard] way" and Delta's "family feeling" convey the sense of being part of a team. The anthropological term *clan* aptly portrays this identification with a social entity (Beer and others, 1985b). Since they share values, risks, and rewards, employees are oriented to collective achievement and thus contribute to goals beyond immediate self-interest. Profit sharing or other means of gain sharing are the rewards most commonly linked with such group or total organization achievement. Ironically, this form of corporate culture is reminiscent of the collegiality traditionally (and perhaps somewhat wistfully) associated with colleges and universities.

As Kanter (1983) points out, corporate leaders are responsible for setting this cultural tone. In outstanding organizations, individuals holding leadership positions have proven capable of generating enthusiasm among employees at all levels (Peters and Waterman, 1982). Personal productivity of these top managers becomes a vital symbol. In corporate enterprises Kanter (1983, p. 146) found that "a combination of relative independence from higher levels and relative interdependence among peers across functions" most effectively fosters initiative. These conditions are not so different from the academic freedom and peer collaboration prized by college and university faculties. Thus, perhaps higher education institutions, too, can benefit from this wide array of incentives used in the corporate world.

Obviously, some types of incentives are more appropriate for the campus setting than others. Monetary incentives such as salary increases, bonuses, and grants clearly prove applicable, whereas pins, buttons, and badges do not. Few self-respecting faculty members would don a badge to mark a recently published article. However, school or campus-wide publications can note such events, and faculty books and articles may be prominently displayed in the school or library. Special teaching and research awards can also heighten morale and encourage excellence, particularly when presented as part of an important ceremonial occasion. The variety of incentives available to a college or university is limited only by an institution's collective imagination and its range of resources.

Relative Nature of Incentives. In order to derive the maximum benefit from incentives such as those just described, colleges and universities must apply them appropriately. For instance, incentives have a relative or contextual nature that can affect their impact. What motivates one professor may not motivate another. In fact, what motivates a professor at one time or in one circumstance may prove totally ineffective in a different situation. An institution has little control over the value a person places on the incentives it offers. The value attached to any particular reward or other type of incentive is largely a function of the person's particular circumstances and needs (Porter and others, 1975).

Certainly professors' disciplines and fields of specialization comprise an element of the complex incentive equation. Important differences among the faculty subcultures defined by academic disciplines and professional fields result in differing values and norms. Tuckman (1979) concludes from his study of the academic reward system that faculty members are subject to a different relative set of incentives, depending on the field they are in. In other words, what fosters the performance of chemists will not necessarily foster the effective performance of visual artists or anthropologists. For example, institutional policies that encourage collaboration with local businesses and community agencies may stimulate the creative talents of a professor of business but would do very little to motivate a professor of philosophy.

The types and missions of academic institutions are also related to the incentive issue. The various colleges and universities select professors with somewhat differing interests and skills. Likewise, they have differing expectations of effective faculty performance. Hence the incentives various types of institutions employ and the incentives their faculty members respond to sometimes reflect special values and goals. For this reason, the incentives that will support faculty vitality in a liberal arts college are not always the same incentives that will support vitality in a research university. Colleges and universities need to structure incentives that are directly relevant to their institutional goals and to the needs of the professors they employ.

Developmental differences among professors may also influence the potency of incentives. (Lawrence addresses this issue in Chapter Five of this volume.) Baldwin and Blackburn (1981) report that professors' interests and desires for various types of work change over the course of the academic career. McKeachie (1979) concludes from motivation theory that individuals at different stages of life assign different values to potential satisfactions. These conclusions suggest that an incentive such as a fund to support the travel of faculty members who present papers at professional association meetings might foster the productivity of a novice college teacher. However, the incentive would not necessarily be equally invigorating to a midlife professor who is longing to move his career in a new direction. Incentives that are insensitive to professor's developmental differences are likely to be less than fully effective.

Tuckman (1979) provides concrete evidence of the differential value of incentives at successive career stages. He argues that incentives for productivity are strongest early in the academic career because professional accomplishments at that stage contribute to promotion and open up future career options for young professors. He shows that economic incentives for achievement are also strongest early in the career, since they typically increase a professor's base salary. Tuckman demonstrates that the later in life a salary increment occurs, the lower its dollar value.

Tuckman's point is that the incentive system in colleges and universities is typically balanced in favor of those with a long work life ahead of them. In contrast, professors later in their careers have fewer incentives for further productivity. Tuckman's analysis of the academic reward structure implies that as professors age, some incentives for them to remain vital contributors to their institutions and disciplinary fields diminish.

Important individual differences among faculty members can also influence the impact of various incentives. Research indicates considerable individual variation in the degree to which rewards are valued (Porter and others, 1975). Members of the academic profession do not constitute a homogeneous group. Some evidence suggests that faculty differences in terms of interests, abilities, and roles are likely to increase over time (McKeachie, 1984). The existence of significant individual differences makes it unwise to apply incentives purely categorically. Personnel policy makers may wish to design incentives for professors in certain disciplines. Similarly, it may be beneficial to target incentives at professors in particular stages of their academic careers. However, the most important factor is to consider professors individually and to offer incentives that most appropriately respond to their unique interests and needs.

Conclusion

Challenging conditions in colleges and universities have focused increased attention on the faculty members who will determine the course of higher education for the remainder of this century. It is clear that energetic, resourceful professors committed to their institutions and to quality education will be necessary to meet the growing demands for innovative and flexible academic programs.

These same conditions have also focused greater attention on colleges and universities as employers and work places. This attention has demonstrated that institutions of higher learning are exciting places to work, places where people continually grow and create. However, greater scrutiny has also shown that many professors gradually lose their initial spark of vitality in the academic work environment, and their effectiveness as professionals eventually falters. Many other academics fail to realize their full potential in a personnel system that does not adequately foster their special talents. Careful inspection of the academic work place has demonstrated the short-sighted and idiosyncratic nature of much faculty personnel policy (Clark and Lewis, 1985).

To meet the educational demands of the future, higher education institutions must offer personnel policies and a comprehensive work environment that not only encourage but indeed compel faculty members to perform at the highest levels of excellence. To achieve this goal, colleges and universities must devise incentives that call forth the best efforts of every member of their faculties. As the brief survey of corporate incentives has indicated, colleges and universities have a wide range of techniques at their disposal. However, they must craft incentives that acknowledge the special nature of academic employment, that capitalize on the rewards intrinsic to academic life, and that are sensitive to the special values and unique circumstances of professors from various disciplines and career stages. Finally, institutions of higher education must create a mixture of incentives sufficiently broad to stimulate the morale and performance of a highly diverse group of talented individuals.

Too often in the past, incentives have not been employed effectively. Academic administrators and faculty personnel committees have frequently failed to outline systematic strategies for utilizing incentives. Many times they have not offered incentives when they would be most effective. In other cases they have not applied incentives in the consistent manner necessary to maintain continuous professional growth and achievement. Perhaps most unfortunate, higher education institutions have often failed to design incentives that respond to the distinctive needs of their professors or that support their institution's special mission and goals.

Colleges and universities wishing to derive the maximum benefit from incentives should carefully tailor them to local circumstances. An incentive that works well at Harvard will not necessarily work well at Hiram College or at Youngstown State. Considerable self-examination is required to custom design a work environment that fosters faculty vitality. As they pursue this objective, colleges and universities should repeatedly ask themselves the following questions:

1. What is our primary educational mission?

18

2. Where do we want our institution to be five, ten, fifteen years from now?
3. Who are our faculty members?
4. What are their strengths, weaknesses, and special needs?
5. What types of incentives will best support our goals?
6. Which incentives are likely to have the greatest and longest-lasting impact on our faculty members?
7. What combination of incentives can we afford to offer?

Educational resources—economic, physical, and human—are too precious to waste. Thoughtful answers to questions of this sort will help higher education institutions develop incentives that will most effectively support the performance and renewal of their most important resource—their faculty members.

References

Austin, A. E., and Gamson, Z. T. *Academic Workplace: New Demands, Heightened Tensions.* ASHE-ERIC Higher Education Research Report, No. 10. Washington, D.C.: Association for the Study of Higher Education, 1983.
Baldwin, R. G., and Blackburn, R. T. "The Academic Career as a Developmental Process: Implications for Higher Education." *Journal of Higher Education,* 1981, *52* (6), 598–614.
Beer, M., Spector, B., Lawrence, P. R., Mills, D. Q., and Walton, R. E. "Managing Human Assets: Part 1." *Personnel Administrator,* 1985a, *30* (1), 60–69.
Beer, M., Spector, B., Lawrence, P. R., Mills, D. Q., and Walton, R. E. "Managing Human Assets: Part 2." *Personnel Administrator,* 1985b, *30* (2), 78–85.
Blackburn, R. T. "Academic Careers: Patterns and Possibilities." *Current Issues in Higher Education,* 1979, *2,* 25–27.
Blackburn, R. T., and Baldwin, R. G. "Faculty as Human Resources: Reality and Potential." In R. G. Baldwin and R. T. Blackburn (Eds.), *College Faculty: Versatile Human Resources in a Period of Constraint.* New Directions for Institutional Research, no. 40, San Francisco: Jossey-Bass, 1983.
Business-Higher Education Forum. *America's Business Schools: Priorities for Change.* Washington, D.C.: Business-Higher Education Forum, 1985.
Centra, J. A. "Maintaining Faculty Vitality Through Faculty Development." In S. M. Clark and D. R. Lewis (Eds.), *Faculty Vitality and Institutional Productivity: Critical Perspectives for Higher Education.* New York: Teachers College, Columbia University, 1985.
Clark, S. M., and Corcoran, M. "Individual and Organizational Contributions to Faculty Vitality: An Institutional Case Study." In S. M. Clark and D. R. Lewis (Eds.), *Faculty Vitality and Institutional Productivity: Critical Perspectives for Higher Education.* New York: Teachers College, Columbia University, 1985.
Clark, S. M., and Lewis, D. R. "Implications for Institutional Response." In S. M. Clark and D. R. Lewis (Eds.), *Faculty Vitality and Institutional Productivity: Critical Perspectives for Higher Education.* New York: Teachers College, Columbia University, 1985.
Clark, S. M., Boyer, C. M., and Corcoran, M. "Faculty and Institutional Vitality in Higher Education." In S. M. Clark and D. R. Lewis (Eds.), *Faculty Vitality and Institutional Productivity: Critical Perspectives for Higher Education.* New York: Teachers College, Columbia University, 1985.

Finkelstein, M. J. "Faculty Colleagueship Patterns and Research Productivity." Paper presented at the annual meeting of the American Educational Research Association, New York, March 1982.

Finkelstein, M. J. *The American Academic Profession: A Synthesis of Social Scientific Inquiry Since World War II.* Columbus: Ohio State University Press, 1984.

Finn, C. E. "Trying Higher Education: An Eight-Count Indictment." *Change,* 1984, *16* (4), 28–33, 47–51.

Frye, B. E. "Observations on Academic Renewal." In M. Waggoner, R. Alfred, and M. Peterson (Eds.), *Academic Renewal: Advancing Higher Education Toward the Nineties.* Ann Arbor: The University of Michigan, School of Education, 1984.

Gardner, J. W. *Morale.* New York: Norton, 1978.

Halcrow, A. "The Lockheed Diet." *Personnel Journal,* 1985, *64* (2), 24–25.

Kanter, R. M. "Changing the Shape of Work: Reform in Academe." *Current Issues in Higher Education,* 1979, *1,* 3–9.

Kanter, R. M. *The Change Masters: Innovations for Productivity in the American Corporation.* New York: Simon and Schuster, 1983.

Keller, G. *Academic Strategy: The Management Revolution in American Higher Education.* Baltimore, Md.: Johns Hopkins University Press, 1983.

McKeachie, W. J. "Perspectives from Psychology: Financial Incentives Are Ineffective for Faculty." In D. R. Lewis and W. E. Becker, Jr. (Eds.), *Academic Rewards in Higher Education.* Cambridge, Mass.: Ballinger, 1979.

McKeachie, W. J. "Enhancing Productivity in Postsecondary Education." *Journal of Higher Education,* 1982, *53* (4), 460–464.

McKeachie, W. J. "The Faculty as a Renewable Resource." In M. Waggoner, R. Alfred, and M. Peterson (Eds.), *Academic Renewal: Advancing Higher Education Toward the Nineties.* Ann Arbor: The University of Michigan, School of Education, 1984.

MacMillan, I. C., and Schuler, R. S. "Gaining a Competitive Edge Through Human Resources." *Personnel,* 1985, *62* (4), 24–29.

Marcaccio, T. M. "Incentives to Sell Your Sales Team." *Personnel Journal,* 1985, *64* (1), 45–47.

Mayo, E. *The Human Problems of an Industrial Civilization.* New York: Macmillan, 1933.

Peters, T. J., and Waterman, R. H. *In Search of Excellence: Lessons from America's Best-Run Companies.* New York: Harper & Row, 1982.

Porter, L. W., Lawler, E. E., and Hackman, J. R. *Behavior in Organizations.* New York: McGraw-Hill, 1975.

Printz, R. A., and Waldman, D. A. "The Merit of Merit Pay." *Personnel Administrator,* 1985, *30* (1), 84–90.

Smith, D. K. "Faculty Vitality and the Management of University Personnel Policies." In W. R. Kirschling (Ed.), *Evaluating Faculty Performance and Vitality.* New Directions for Institutional Research, no. 20. San Francisco: Jossey-Bass, 1978.

Tuckman, H. P. "The Academic Reward Structure in American Higher Education." In D. R. Lewis and W. E. Becker, Jr. (Eds.), *Academic Rewards in Higher Education.* Cambridge, Mass.: Ballinger, 1979.

Veysey, L. R. *The Emergence of the American University.* Chicago: The University of Chicago Press, 1965.

Roger G. Baldwin is assistant professor of higher education at the College of William and Mary, in Williamsburg, Virginia. His research focuses on the academic work place and the career development of college professors.

Marsha V. Krotseng is a doctoral candidate and research assistant at the College of William and Mary. Her research interests include public policy, the state's role in higher education, and organizational careers.

Professors themselves assess the conditions conducive to a vital faculty.

Faculty Vitality: Observations from the Field

Jack H. Schuster

What are the correlates of faculty vitality? And what can a college or university do to stimulate and facilitate faculty vitality? These are among the most important questions confronting American higher education at a time when constrained resources, a "greying," tenured professoriate, and deepening anxiety about the proximate future combine to limit institutional flexibility and dampen faculty esprit. This chapter describes and assesses observations about faculty vitality drawn from a wide-ranging study of the American professoriate. The ensuing sections, in turn, provide a context for the findings that are reported, identify a number of conditions associated with faculty vitality, draw some conclusions from those findings, and suggest several strategies that can be useful in the promotion of a vital faculty.

In addition to the author, interviewers were E. Howard Brooks, Claremont McKenna College; Martin J. Finkelstein, Seton Hall University; Patricia J. Foster, Loma Linda University; and Wilbert J. McKeachie, University of Michigan, Ann Arbor.

R. G. Baldwin (Ed.). *Incentives for Faculty Vitality.* New Directions for
Higher Education, no. 51. San Francisco: Jossey-Bass, September 1985.

A Note on Context

Over the past several years I have collaborated with my colleague, Howard Bowen, in an effort to assess the condition of America's faculties. Our concern, from the outset, was that working conditions that affect the quality of academic life are in decline, possibly even sharp decline. Thus, we wanted to learn what we could about the consequences—or, at least, the perceived consequences—of these changing conditions for the vitality of the faculty. We were equally concerned about the extent to which these changes in the work place might impair the ability of colleges and universities to attract highly able people to academic careers.

We found, in general, that conditions affecting American faculty have been deteriorating. Both compensation (after adjustments for inflation) and the quality of the work environment have declined sharply over the past decade or so. Faculty morale appeared to us on the whole to be shaky; although in respectably decent shape at the stronger research universities and liberal arts colleges, faculty morale was weak, sometimes dismally low, at some of the campuses caught up in severe financial straits. We also found that higher education is having an increasingly difficult time attracting highly able young people to academic careers (Bowen and Schuster, 1986).

These conclusions are derived in part from a series of campus visits undertaken between November 1983 and May 1984. Specifically, this aspect of our investigation entailed visits to thirty-eight campuses, during which six researchers conducted a total of 532 semi-structured interviews: 225 with rank-and-file faculty members, 127 with department chairs (primarily in biology, history, physics, and political science), and 180 with higher-level administrators having some responsibility for academic affairs (predominantly presidents, provosts, and academic deans).

To place in perspective our findings as they relate to faculty vitality, it is important to understand the kinds of questions we raised. Our overarching objective was to understand our respondents' perceptions of the quality of faculty life and the extent to which work-place conditions have been changing over the past decade and a half. To accomplish this, several of the questions in our thirty-two-item interview guide were intended to elicit opinions about such broad and rather vague concepts as the status of faculty morale and collegiality. Thus, to illustrate, we asked: How would you describe the state of faculty morale on this campus? and, Has faculty morale changed significantly here over the past five to ten years?

Other questions were more pointed; they sought out faculty and administrative opinions about particular aspects of faculty life. These items ranged, for example, from questions about faculty earnings from outside the campus to the caliber of newly hired faculty, from the implications of a "greying" professoriate to changes in standards for obtaining tenure, from faculty housing costs to the consequences of shifting academic interests among students and changes in their preparedness for college.

Focusing on Faculty Vitality. Two questions specifically addressed the issue of faculty vitality. One three-part question asked: What in your opinion are the ingredients that create faculty vitality? What specifically is being done at this institution to facilitate or restore faculty vitality? and What should be done at this institution to facilitate faculty vitality? Another question was one of a series intended to evoke opinions on the quality of graduate students and young faculty members. We asked: Are high-quality graduate students critical to the vitality of your faculty? [And if so] In what ways?

Two further contextual matters are worth noting. First, not all respondents were asked all the questions; various questions were targeted for specific categories of respondents. Thus, the analysis that follows is based on the recorded responses of somewhat fewer than half of our 532 interviewees. I have attempted in the following pages to glean from those responses both the most representative and the most insightful comments. Second, no effort was made to provide respondents with a precise definition of *faculty vitality.* A term so general no doubt meant different things to different respondents. While definitions of faculty vitality abound (Clark and others, 1985), I was attracted to the formulation suggested by the head of one of the community colleges we visited: "Vitality," she said, "is an inner quality of individuals who go beyond the parameters of their job descriptions only because they want to." The following discussion is largely an effort to identify the campus conditions, based on what faculty members and administrators told us, that would motivate individual faculty members to stretch beyond the parameters of their job descriptions.

The Correlates of Faculty Vitality

Our respondents identified numerous elements that they associated with faculty vitality. I have arbitrarily constructed two categories of factors that bear on the degree to which a faculty is or is not "vital." I view the first group of factors as being tangible. They are, in a sense, goods or services. The second cluster of factors is attitudinal; I call them the intangibles. I do not contend that the two groups of factors are wholly distinguishable; several items spill across this arbitrary boundary, but on the whole the suggested division, like that of other suggested schema (Blackburn and Baldwin, 1983), may serve a useful purpose.

The Tangibles. The tangibles are the most obvious factors. They all bear directly on faculty working conditions. And they all cost money. The result is a familiar litany of needs, which I have organized under five headings:

The Tools of Research. A vital faculty is one that has at hand the means to conduct research. This translates into library holdings and laboratories with adequate space and contemporary equipment. Little elaboration is needed here, but some perspective on the differing needs of faculty members is reflected in the observation of an arts and sciences dean at a research university: "I don't guess there's anything that takes the place of money. For the hard scientists, though, state-of-the-art equipment is critical."

The Means for Intellectual Refreshment. In this era of compressed institutional budgets, the support necessary to enable faculty members to attend professional meetings is frequently mentioned. One graduate dean put it concisely: "Getting away on a periodic basis is very important to this faculty." Sabbatical leaves are frequently identified as a crucial ingredient of faculty vitality. Although under scrutiny at a number of institutions we visited, sabbatical leaves appear not to have been seriously curtailed. On several campuses the opinion was voiced that a more keenly competitive sabbatical leave policy, rather than one in which leaves accrue solely as a function of time in service, would encourage more intellectual liveliness.

The Stimulation of Good Students. The faculty members and administrators whom we interviewed embraced the objective of having good students as a means of promoting faculty vitality. They used such expressions as: a high-caliber student body, alert students, challenging, demanding, and intellectually interesting students.

We inquired about the importance of high-quality graduate students at the fifteen institutions in our sample that offered doctoral programs. Many of our respondents at these institutions asserted emphatically that good graduate students were essential for keeping the faculty intellectually engaged. A dean at a prominent research university went so far as to say that "we couldn't exist without them." An engineering dean at another university maintained that "the faculty we attract come here to do research and to work with graduate students; without quality graduate students, they wouldn't stay."

Sometimes the case for excellent graduate students is made on the grounds that their lively or motivated or probing behavior requires faculty to be alert in order "to keep up." More often, the importance of graduate students is linked directly to faculty productivity, especially in the natural sciences. One respondent explained it simply: "Because productivity is measured by the amount of good work in the laboratory, graduate students (or postdoctorates) are extremely important." One dean of a science division described graduate students this way: "They are the life blood of the faculty's professional career." A further rationale—probably widely appreciated if not commonly articulated—was suggested by one historian: "If we were left just to our own colleagues, the faculty would just go crazy."

The importance of good graduate students was emphasized in one further way. At several institutions—but not at the most esteemed research universities—concern was expressed about a perceived decline in the quality of doctoral students. The chair of one science department lamented, "It's our biggest problem." One arts and sciences dean perhaps summed it up best: "They share your interest; they are the future."

Relief from a Too-Arduous Work Load. Faculty members, quite predictably, suggested that their vitality was dependent on a manageable work load. The usual target was a teaching load deemed unconscionably heavy. But administrators, too, at research universities and small colleges alike, recognized the importance of a teaching load that was "reasonable" or "proper." Budgeting necessities may have kept teaching loads uncomfortably high at some institutions, but at least one academic vice-president at a liberal arts college stressed the critical importance of providing periodic relief from a heavy teaching schedule; she underscored the need to give faculty members a lower teaching load on a rotating basis.

The Symbolism (and Security) of Compensation. In one sense, compensation ought not to be discussed only as a tangible factor, though we realize that a monthly bank deposit is indisputably tangible. A vital faculty, as pointed out to us time and again, is one that is not obliged to be preoccupied with the rudiments of economic survival. (More than a few faculty members, particularly at some of the nonprospering liberal arts colleges we visited, stressed how much of their energy had been diverted into providing for their families.) But beyond those fundamental economic concerns that had beset some faculty members, the symbolic importance of compensation loomed large. Neither was its symbolic significance lost on the faculty or administrators. As one university president observed, faculty members must feel they are being rewarded. One historian put it this way: "Faculty pay indicates how we are esteemed" (and he added that it was not difficult to demonstrate that historians were not well esteemed at his campus!). A faculty committee at a highly respected liberal arts college, believing that the faculty had become demoralized by what it deemed inadequate compensation, suggested in a report to the college's trustees that a very direct linkage existed between faculty compensation and a propensity to be active: "It will take generous spirits all around to overcome the salary problem and create an atmosphere of hustle and enthusiasm." I do not assert here that we found that money can buy vitality; indeed, the research literature suggests otherwise (for example, see McKeachie, 1979). But adequate compensation, according to an impressive number of our respondents, enables faculty members to feel good about themselves; without it, they suggest, vitality is hard to come by.

The Intangibles. Compared to the tangible factors just outlined, the intangibles are less obvious. These factors are not so much concrete dimensions of the work place as they are reflections of attitudes toward the faculty. Such attitudes, arguably, are even more important as underpinnings of a vital faculty than the tangible factors are. The observations of those whom we interviewed can be grouped under four headings.

Encouragement by Leadership. Administrative leadership is widely perceived as playing a key role in creating and maintaining the conditions of faculty vitality. Apart from the obvious administrative task of providing adequate resources, from equipment to salaries, two further, distinct administrative roles emerged from our interviews: providing psychological support for faculty and defining institutional direction.

In the realm of demonstrating support, the crucial elements are providing recognition, showing appreciation, and promoting faculty self-esteem. In this regard, a small investment of an administrator's time can pay off handsomely; it is, according to a graduate dean, a matter merely of "the small trouble it takes to recognize people who are doing something." A president commented that it is almost as simple as patting people on the back. One biologist emphasized the importance of instilling the faculty with "a sense of their worth." Stated differently, it is the need to foster in faculty members a sense of their contribution to the whole picture. Perhaps the formulation proffered by a history chair at a state university best sums up the administrative opportunity and responsibility; in his prescription the administrative task is to impart to faculty "a feeling of being needed and respected."

The other administrative imperative associated with faculty vitality is that of providing a clear sense of direction for the institution. At a time of widespread uncertainty about what the future holds for colleges and universities—indeed, the question of survival was a realistic one at some of the institutions we visited—faculty and administrators attest to the importance of clarifying institutional objectives and priorities as one means of fostering a committed faculty. "We need to know what is expected of us," commented one biologist. And a dean of faculty added, "We need a president who is talking about where the president is going."

A Sense of Community. Faculty vitality was seen by many of our respondents as flourishing best when faculty members share a sense that they are part of a single academic community. Large, complex institutions, often decentralized and fragmented, present obstacles to an awareness of community. The administration must transcend organizational fragmentation, as well as the existence of quite different faculty subcultures on a single campus, to establish, in the words of one president of a celebrated university, "the idea that this is one university."

This sense of community depends in some measure on two commonly mentioned conditions: effective faculty participation in the governance process and fairness in decision making. The importance of faculty involvement in governance has been written about extensively and need not be elaborated on here. It may be worth noting, nonetheless, that one provost at a liberal arts college singled out the importance of involving faculty particularly in the college's long-range planning. Interestingly, a faculty member at the same campus noted that the adminstration "must not pressure the faculty into wearing too many hats." Similar caveats, we found, were subscribed to by quite a few faculty members who complained that much of their time was siphoned off into committee work or "administrivia." One professor of business administration boasted: "I haven't seen the dean all semester; it's wonderful!" And the chair of a university physics department observed along those same lines that we "need to protect [the faculty] from nonsense and let them be creative." As in most things, though, the answer lies in finding an appropriate balance. One community college dean we interviewed provided a useful insight: A vital faculty, he suggested, is one that "has the opportunity to influence matters that affect faculty directly."

If meaningful participation is one dimension of a sense of community, fair procedures constitute another. Our interview subjects commonly underscored the importance of fairness and openness in the campus's decision-making processes: "Equitable and even-handed treatment of faculty" is how one dean put it. "A governance structure that faculty can trust," suggests a graduate dean. One political scientist accentuated the importance of the faculty having "a sense that the university is a place where there are no deep, dark secrets."

The Safeguarding of Intellectual Freedom. Faculty members and administrators joined in emphasizing that academic freedom is a condition prerequisite for faculty vitality. One economist ventured further when he asserted that a campus's leadership must in fact "encourage heterodoxy in the views of faculty."

The Stimulation of Colleagues. One further ingredient of faculty vitality bears mention: the importance of colleagues who themselves are possessed of vitality. Perhaps it is nonsensical—or, at the least, circular—to enumerate "vital colleagues" among the correlates of faculty vitality. After all, if one's colleagues are lively and energetic, the faculty is by definition imbued with vitality. But it is a finer point that our respondents made—the notion that creativity begets creativity. Indeed, it is altogether plausible that a faculty can be comfortably situated with better than adequate facilities at hand and be blessed further with a non-onerous work load, a caring administration, and a challenging student body—and still exhibit no discernible spark. Perhaps the most essential ingredient is expressed in the words of a historian at a first-rank university who suggested that faculty vitality depends "on a sense that you are surrounded by people who are creative and energetic." One university department chair defined these elusive qualities as "vision, creativity, and aspiration." A young professor of French at a distinguished liberal arts college was inspired by her college's recruitment of "vital people." The chair of English at one university emphasized the need to restrict academic appointments to "innovative and energetic faculty."

Some Lessons from the Field

What lessons can be derived from this exploration of responses to our questions about faculty vitality? Are there any surprises there? Are the circumstances that are normally assumed to be conducive to a vital faculty essentially the same factors our respondents identified? One is tempted to indulge in a somewhat facetious summary, to declare that the mists that for so long have obscured the pathways to faculty vitality have now been dissipated, revealing the equation for faculty vitality for all to see:

$$A_{cp} + F_l + S_c + AR_{1 \ldots n} = F_v$$

Where A_{cp} is an Administration that cares about the faculty and successfully communicates that care, that provides a purposeful, clear direction for the campus, and that, at the same time, approaches governance with a view toward involving the faculty significantly in the campus's decision-making processes;

Where F_l is a Faculty predisposed and recruited to be lively, to be intellectually acute, and to value colleagueship;

Where S_c is a Student body comprised of challenging undergraduates and (where applicable) highly motivated graduate students;

Where $AR_{1 \ldots n}$ is nothing less than the Adequate Resources (money) to provide a supportive environment (from sabbatical leaves to state-of-the-art instrumentation); and

Where F_v is, of course, a Faculty characterized by vitality.

Surely there are no great surprises here. But if the formulation just made is in some respects merely a restatement of the predictable, several conclusions emerge that may bear emphasizing. Perhaps the paramount lesson is this: It is less difficult to articulate the conditions—both physical and attitudinal—that one associates with faculty vitality than it is to produce these conditions. At least theoretically, the intangible conditions, which in large measure flow from a facilitative attitude on the part of administrators (and trustees), should not be too difficult to come by. It is the tangibles that are expensive. The commitments of trustees, presidents, deans, and department chairs to be supportive of the faculty might be altogether laudable, even inspirational. But that commitment in itself, essential as it may be, does not go far enough. Sufficient resources must also be present if faculty vitality is to be sustained.

One might counter with examples of institutions, possibly church-related or consciously nonconformist, in which faculty zest and commitment know no bounds—despite (or arguably because of) survival-threatening financial conditions. No doubt such places did, and still do, exist. But, at least according to what we were told, inspiring leadership and faculty cohesion alone are inadequate conditions for sustained faculty vitality at the large majority of American colleges and universities. If such is the case, it is clear that the administrative burden is all the more challenging, for not only must the administration help to develop through leadership the ethos of the work environment, the administration must also succeed in marshalling the necessary resources, amid formidable competing demands, to facilitate faculty regeneration.

A corollary to the preceding observation is that financial support can make a big difference in boosting faculty morale and, presumably, in enhancing faculty vitality. Among the campuses we visited were a number that had recently completed, or were nearing completion of, highly ambitious fund-raising campaigns. We heard numerous faculty testaments at those campuses about how much difference the infusion of money made, not only in terms of take-home pay but also in terms of a new esprit among faculty members. The overall conclusion I draw is two-fold: Leadership is critically important in establishing and maintaining the conditions in which faculty vitality can flourish. But inspirational and sensitive leadership that is not reinforced with sufficient tangible resources can hardly be successful by itself.

Two additional and somewhat curious notes: First, it is interesting that our respondents did not point to systematic faculty development programs of one stripe or another as being associated in their minds with the creation or maintenance of faculty vitality. Perhaps that apparent anomaly is attributable to our manner of asking questions. Second, faculty unions were not mentioned, either. The faculties at ten of the thirty-eight campuses in our sample were represented by exclusive bargaining agents. It is interesting that none of the faculty or administrators whom we interviewed on these campuses suggested that faculty unions bear any relationship to faculty vitality.

Strategies for Vitality

In the course of our interviews, several suggestions emerged that I believe deserve some consideration as strategies designed to enhance faculty vitality.

Requiring New Offerings. Deans and department chairs ought to strongly encourage, if not absolutely require, that faculty members not teach precisely the same courses or seminars each year. One means of implementing this strategy is to discourage a faculty member from offering the same course for a fourth (third? fifth?) consecutive year—unless extraordinary circumstances dictate that discontinuation is undesirable. This strategy contemplates that while Professor A is on leave from teaching one of his standard courses, Professor B would be obliged to teach the course, if it is a department staple. Professor A would take on a new offering, and, presumably, both faculty members would benefit from the challenge. Such strategies are not exactly foolproof. I recall the crafty Professor Gold's ploy in Joseph Heller's *Good as*

Gold (1979, pp. 135–138). In order to divert students from competing academic departments, Gold created seductive titles and catalogue descriptions for his colleagues' courses (example: "The Role of Women, Blacks, and Drugs in Sex and Religion in World and American Film and Literature"); students who enrolled in such courses were puzzled to discover that the assigned readings and the content of lectures were indistinguishable from previous offerings, including Gold's well-worn Shakespeare course.

Negotiated Work Load Contracts. A number of institutions have experimented with performance contracting in one form or another. One relatively uncomplicated version is to encourage faculty members to propose variations of their usual assignments. For example, a professor who usually teaches three courses per semester may propose that he or she be released from one of those courses in order to develop a new course or to carry out a particular research project.

Creative Leaves. Designed to supplement regular sabbatical leave policies, a "creative leave" program might provide on a competitive basis the opportunity for faculty members to take leaves of absence to pursue particularly promising creative endeavors. The number of such leaves might be quite small, but even one per semester at, say, a liberal arts college with eighty to one hundred faculty members would likely be of some value in encouraging new intellectual ventures.

Faculty Forums. There are many variations on a faculty-forum theme. The central idea assumes that faculties at both large and small institutions have little understanding of the kinds of intellectual problems and issues that engage their colleagues in other fields. Periodic forums, preferably informal, that enable faculty members to explain their current research (and, with luck, to convey a sense of excitement about it) help to stimulate faculty colleagues.

Assertive Presidential Leadership. Presidents can and do make a difference. This theme surfaced repeatedly in our interviews. Much of the literature on higher education stresses the constraints on effective leadership that stem from a nonhierarchial organizational structure, especially in an era of limited institutional growth, if not outright retrenchment. Yet effective administrative leadership was identified again and again as a crucial precondition for faculty vitality. Accordingly, such simple "programs" as systematic recognition of faculty achievement are very helpful. Similarly, a consultative mode of governance, which emphasizes faculty participation, helps create a proper environment.

Hiring Despite the Numbers. One final strategy deserves lengthier comment. Many of the institutions we visited had done very little hiring of new faculty members in the liberal arts for some time. Furthermore, in many of those instances, few if any new hires were anticipated for some years to come. With the age of retirement having risen as a function of federal legislation, many faculty members face a future of growing older together with slim prospects for infusing their departments with young faculty members. Our interviewees commonly reported that such an outlook tends to depress vitality. We encountered a number of instances where, for example, a history department had recently completed its first search in a decade, or was in the process of hiring a new assistant professor, and we were impressed by the excitement that this generated. These conditions suggested to us that hiring despite the numbers has exciting potential, although it constitutes a controversial approach.

Specifically, a department may find that decreasing enrollments not only do not justify adding academic appointments but, based on student-faculty ratios, may even suggest the need for faculty reductions. Such departments—like the physics department we encountered at an eminent research university—are legion. At the research university, the faculty felt keenly the need to hire young, freshly trained faculty members, especially since no new faculty members had been hired for a decade. A number of physicists were scheduled to retire during the next six to ten years, and this situation provided the conditions for an imaginative bargain between the department and the administration. The department sought, and obtained, authorization to hire at the assistant professor level—not just one but a half-dozen young faculty members over the next several years. In return, the department acknowledged that these new hires would be replacements for the faculty nearing retirement age, which is to say, the department would not press to replace the older faculty members when they did retire. The result appears to be that a distinguished department that had lost some of its zest had adopted a strategy designed for revitalization. And the administration agreed to this bold approach, although it meant having to fend off requests from other academic departments that had legitimate claims, based on current enrollments, for some of those precious academic positions that were awarded to the physics department. This strategy has considerably wide applicability.

Conclusion

In the course of our interviews, the role of administrators in promoting faculty vigor emerged with unexpected salience. In the words of one university dean, the key is the signal from the administration that "it believes the faculty's role to be the most important one in the university." That attitude "filters down from above," observed another dean, "from the president through the department chairs to the individual faculty members."

No single approach to faculty regeneration can succeed everywhere, for institutional characteristics and faculty cultures vary so much from one setting to another. Nonetheless, as American colleges and universities strive to meet the challenges of maintaining quality despite constrained resources,

32

the single most important element for ensuring faculty vitality is surely vigorous, purposeful, sensitive campus administration.

References

Blackburn, R. T., and Baldwin, R. G. "Faculty as Human Resources: Reality and Potential." In R. G. Baldwin and R. T. Blackburn (Eds.), *College Faculty: Versatile Human Resources in a Period of Constraint.* New Directions for Institutional Research, no. 40. San Francisco: Jossey-Bass, 1983.
Bowen, H. R., and Schuster, J. H. *American Professors: A National Resource Imperiled.* New York: Oxford University Press, 1986.
Clark, S. M., Boyer, C. M, and Corcoran, M. "Faculty and Institutional Vitality in Higher Education." In S. M. Clark and D. R. Lewis (Eds.), *Faculty Vitality and Institutional Productivity: Critical Perspectives for Higher Education.* New York: Teachers College, Columbia University, 1985.
Heller, J. *Good as Gold.* New York: Simon and Schuster, 1979.
McKeachie, W. J. "Financial Incentives Are Ineffective for Faculty." In D. R. Lewis and W. E. Becker, Jr. (Eds.), *Academic Rewards in Higher Education.* Cambridge, Mass.: Ballinger, 1979.

Jack H. Schuster is associate professor of education and public policy at The Claremont Graduate School, where he directs the graduate program in higher education. He is coauthor with Howard R. Bowen of American Professors: A National Resource Imperiled.

Ideally, incentives for faculty vitality are mutually supportive and give rise spontaneously to other incentives.

Faculty Incentives: Some Practical Keys and Practical Examples

Zeddie Bowen

What do we expect of the faculty, and why does it take special incentive in order for these expectations to be met? These questions are good starting points for considering programs of incentives for faculty vitality. Our answers depend on our philosophy of educational leadership, on the realities of faculty life at our individual institutions, and on our goals. Do we expect faculty members to be effective and conscientious teachers, productive and respected scholars, caring and available advisers, helpful and cooperative colleagues? Do we expect them to be creative and innovative, exciting and enthusiastic? Do we expect them to be excellent in all things? For the most part, the answer to all these questions is yes. Within the scope of our expectations may lie the answer to the second question, "Why does it take special incentive?"

Faculty members at the University of Richmond (where the emphasis is on undergraduate teaching, and the standard teaching load is four courses per semester) were asked recently to itemize the ways in which they spend their professional time during a typical week. The results, shown in Table 1, illustrate a major limitation to developing effective incentives. Faculty

R. G. Baldwin (Ed.). *Incentives for Faculty Vitality.* New Directions for
Higher Education, no. 51. San Francisco: Jossey-Bass, September 1985.

34

Table 1. A Typical Work Week Reported By University of
Richmond Faculty

Hours	Activity
11	Teaching in the classroom
20	Preparation for classes and grading papers
7	Student consultations and advising
7	University service: Administrative and quasi-administrative duties, committees, and so on
11	Creativity and innovation: teaching and scholarship
5	Other: Professional societies, consulting, and so on
61	Total Hours

members reported spending long work weeks devoted to their various responsibilities. Whether accurate or not, and I believe that they are for most faculty members, these perceptions set boundaries for successful incentive programs. Any program ignoring faculty's perception that they are already overextended or that time for new ventures falls low on the list of priorities set by the institution, is likely to fail. The first practical key to incentives for faculty vitality is: Do not have unrealistic expectations. Nine other useful and practical keys in setting the context for creating incentives for faculty vitality are described in the rest of this chapter.

Although we recognize both day-to-day and long-term priorities for the faculty, the day-to-day schedule of classes, class preparation, paper grading, advising, committee meetings, and so on leaves little time or energy for the long-term priorities of scholarship, curriculum and course development, and innovative approaches to teaching or for recharging one's intellectual batteries. To establish effective incentives for change, the priorities must be reset, and the incentives, direct and indirect, tangible and intangible, must be designed to reinforce the new priorities. Placing the desired activity nearer the top requires some other activity to be displaced downward or off the list. The second practical key is: Renegotiate the priorities, do not just add new expectations, so that each individual can see how the new priority is to be accommodated in the day-to-day schedule. In successful negotiations, as well as in successful faculty development programs, both parties benefit!

In addition to feeling that they are already overcommitted, faculty members in my experience also perceive that they are doing a good job and deserve a merit increase in salary, at least a small one. Because of this perception of good work, positive results rarely occur when negative faculty evaluations are used to motivate change. We are more likely to change because we want to change than because we have to change or are told to change. The third key, then, is: Create incentives that build on positives, on personal wants rather than needs.

What motivates faculty members? For the most part, we have entered higher education as professionals because of our success as students and our enjoyment of the collegial life-style of the teacher, scholar, and intellectual. We value learning for its own sake and want to be respected and recognized for our knowledge and expertise, commodities that we willingly share with others. We value having great flexibility in the use of our time and the opportunity to follow our own intellectual interests wherever they take us. If these are our primary professional motivations, then the most effective incentives are ones that address these areas. The fourth key is: Tie the incentives to the primary motivators of the faculty.

Incentives differ according to their goals. Where the goals are specific and finite, the incentives should be also. For example, the acquisition of a new skill or body of knowledge, such as that required for a mathematician to teach computer science, can be encouraged by support for the learning experience and subsequent salary adjustments once the new teaching assignment begins. Where the goals are less specific and finite, the right incentives may be harder to identify. Often the goal is to modify attitudes and behavior or to spark enthusiasm or renew energy. Incentive programs can effectively induce behavior modification, but not energy renewal. If the goal is to modify behavior, the key (number five) is: Tie specific and clearly defined goals or changes in behavior to specific and clearly defined rewards, which should be delivered as soon as the desired goal or behavior occurs. Special care must be taken in designing the rewards when behavior modification is the goal because the rewards must be repeated in order to reinforce the behavior change.

While our general motivators may be similar, we respond differently to rewards. If everyone receives the same reward, we may miss unnecessarily the best incentives for some individuals. The sixth key: Individualize the incentives. Be flexible enough to respond to each person. If it is not clear what the individual preferences are, ask.

Incentives may also take on more value if the individual has some choice or control. What difference does it make if the money used for incentives goes for travel, books, equipment, films, guest speakers, luncheons, or whether it is used immediately or saved for an upcoming sabbatical? Probably none. To the faculty member involved, it may mean a great deal and so may the power to choose! The seventh key: Empower the recipient to use the incentives or rewards however and whenever it best suits him or her.

I have found it important to distinguish between basic faculty rights and opportunities. The faculty has a basic right to a fair wage, a reasonable place to work and teach, and a right to be treated with dignity and respect. Such rights should be given to all and denied to none. Participation in an incentive program, however, is an opportunity, not a right. Of course, being selected for such an opportunity can have positive or negative effects. It will have negative effects if it is viewed as a response to the participant's shortcomings. As mentioned earlier, incentives are more effective when built on positives and personal wants rather than needs. In addition, being selected for participation in a positive and competitive program carries with it a special honor and obligation to perform. The eighth key to effective faculty incentive programs is: Make programs selective and somewhat exclusive. It is easier to hold an individual accountable if he or she is participating in a selective incentive program.

Accountability is important. It maintains the integrity and value of the program, the participant, and the administration. If goals cannot be clearly defined and reasonable and objective measures of achievement agreed on by the participant and the administration, perhaps the goals are not worthy of support. If the goals are clearly defined and reasonable and objective measures of achievement are agreed on, then both parties are served well by being held accountable. The integrity and self-esteem that come from honoring a worthwhile contract are only part of the benefit. Accountability motivates! Too often we do not take the time to define the goals and measures and thus never know if they have been achieved. The ninth key is: Define the goals and measures and hold individuals accountable for reasonable achievement. Define the administration's role with equal care and emphasize the importance of its being accountable for upholding its part of the contract.

One last key. We all know about ideas whose time has not yet come. The same is true for some faculty incentives efforts. Before starting, question how serious the problem is, how great the need for change is, how widely the need is recognized, and what the likelihood of achieving the desired goal is. The tenth practical key is: Be sure the goal is worthy of the time and expense. If it is not, abandon it.

The Incentives

Incentives take a variety of forms, tangible and intangible, direct and indirect. Some examples are shown in Table 2.

Direct and Tangible. Monetary incentives of a direct nature play a major role in most faculty incentive programs. Merit pay is an emotionally charged example. When average salary increases do not keep up with inflation, incentive programs may be counterproductive, and initiative, self-respect, and vitality may be eroded in the average faculty member. With this caveat in mind, other direct and tangible incentives can be effective in supporting activities that vitalize the faculty.

Grants for research, equipment, software, data bases, books, and so on are widely used and are successful incentives. Support for faculty travel for research, professional meetings, and workshops are equally popular because they reinforce primary motivations to teach, learn, and be recognized for

Table 2. Varieties of Incentives

Tangible

Direct	*Indirect*
Merit pay	Facilities
Teaching and research grants for books, equipment, travel, and so forth	Equipment
	Libraries
Secretarial and technical assistance	Faculty club

Intangible

Direct	*Indirect*
Tenure	Faculty forum
Promotion	Student research symposium
Sabbaticals	Visiting professors
"Release time"	Outside speakers
Workshops and other learning experiences	Quality of faculty
Responsibility and authority	Quality of students
Recognition	

intellectual achievement. Since these incentives are direct, tangible, and repeatable, they are easy to employ as tools of behavior modification and lend themselves to agreements on accountability. While there are many creative grant programs, several examples, each with a slightly different emphasis, illustrate their versatility.

Small research grant programs funded by institutional resources are found at most colleges and universities. In many cases they are administered by faculty-elected committees. When accountability is taken seriously, faculty-administered programs have the added advantage of peer pressure for performance. Such a program exists at the College of William and Mary, in Virginia, where an added incentive is created by giving back to the committee a portion of the grant overhead income generated by externally supported grants. The committee allocates these funds in the form of new faculty grants in the internally funded grant program.

Less commonly funded by institutional resources are small grants for teaching enhancement. The Program for the Enhancement of Teaching Effectiveness at the University of Richmond makes such grants. Created by the faculty to encourage discussion and reflection about teaching and to foster the faculty's efforts to be the most effective teachers they can be, the faculty-elected committee, using university-budgeted funds, conducts three or four workshops per year, encourages team consultations among peers, and awards small grants to promote understanding and mastery of, or to establish better conditions for the practice of, the craft of teaching. While it does not fund research or travel to professional meetings or workshops aimed at mastery of subject matter, it takes a broad view of pedagogy and asks: Will this project advance this teacher's ability to communicate the information pertinent to his or her discipline?

Many institutions have acquired underendowed chairs or professor-ships whose incomes are insufficient to fund the salary and special perquisites for the holder. Yet being named to a chair is a positive incentive, and the opportunity to use it as such should not be lost. A number of these positions exist at the University of Richmond, where a special effort has been made to provide effective incentives for faculty achievement over a period of years. Each chair holder is nominated by his or her peers, holds the chair for a six-year tenure and receives special perquisites each of those six years. The standard award for such chair holders is an annual stipend (currently set at $3,000) to support teaching and research, only a portion of which may be used for salary enhancement, with the remainder to be used for support of scholarly activities. The availability of these funds, which can be used only at the discretion of the chair holder and only on scholarly activities, is a strong incentive. At Richmond, the funds may also be accumulated by the chair holder over a period of years to support a larger scholarly project at a later date. The flexibility of the funds and the control given to the individual add to their value as an incentive.

Another popular incentive program at the University of Richmond, embodying both tangible and intangible benefits, is a shared purchase arrangement with members of the faculty to buy personal microcomputers. Under this plan, the university will pay half of the cost of a microcomputer for faculty members who agree to pay for the other half. A faculty member's share may be paid through an interest-free payroll deduction for two years, and after five years, the university's share is given to the participant. Each unit is equipped with a printer, extended memory, and a sophisticated word-processing program. Choice of microcomputers is limited (DEC Rainbow 100, IBM PC, Apple IIc and IIe, and MacIntosh) in order to stimulate faculty interaction in interdisciplinary users' groups and to simplify staff support for training and maintenance. The machines may be used at home or in the office or lab at the participant's discretion. Staff support for training and maintenance is provided by the university. Because university funds for this program are limited, not every faculty member can participate, and a degree of competition results. A panel of faculty members and deans participates in choosing from among the applicants. In the first two years of the program, nearly half of the regular faculty members participated.

Why is this program successful? It requires significant commitment on the part of both the participant and the university. Because each participant pays well over $1,000 of his or her own money, there is a high incentive to learn to use the microcomputer for teaching and scholarship. Likewise, the university's investment in the equipment is an effective incentive to follow up with training sessions and support for users' groups. The goals of the program are significant to both the university and the faculty. There is distinction in being selected for participation—pride in mastering something new and adding to one's expertise—and there is the long-term benefit of time saved by the faculty through the use of word processing to produce the vital but mundane products of good teaching, such as up-to-date syllabuses, reading lists, and other materials.

By having control over where the machine is located, each faculty member may choose to work at home in a less threatening environment. For many, the equipment also proves more convenient to use at home. The university has also supplied most academic offices with compatible equipment and letter-quality printers, so that work done on an individual faculty microcomputer can be finished or refined by a secretary. (Note that many of the keys for creating effective faculty incentives mentioned earlier can be brought into play by a program of this sort.)

To the collegiality generated by faculty from different disciplines working together on a common interest, the use of microcomputers is also a positive benefit. The mutual support of colleagues reinforces the significance of the goal. In addition, the machines themselves have stimulated new ways of thinking in several disciplines. One of these disciplines, the teaching of freshman English, illustrates another type of incentive for faculty development.

Another type of institutional grant sometimes thought of as an incentive for excellence in teaching is an award for teacher-, scholar-, or educator-of-the-year. For the few who receive them, the rewards are well earned, but the awards are often regarded poorly by the faculty and do little to inspire greater vitality. More a lottery than an incentive, these awards fail because they do not offer the expected rewards for reasonable accomplishments toward realistic goals. After all, if the reward goes only to the best, all but one fail. Such rewards work best as symbolic testimony to the value we all place on good teaching and good scholarship; by recognizing one (or a few), we symbolically recognize all good teachers and scholars.

A final type of direct and tangible incentive for the faculty is secretarial and technical assistance. Someone once told me research is 10 percent inspiration and 90 percent perspiration, and I agree. If we want faculty members to be creative and feel inspired, secretarial or technical help with the less creative aspects of the work can provide the extra time needed for the main task. Consider how much a faculty member could accomplish if he or she had a secretary one day or even half a day a week for the semester. Where would administrators be without such help?

Direct and Intangible. The impact of intangible incentives should not be underestimated. Tenure (security), promotion (recognition), and sabbaticals (free time to pursue one's own special professional development) are the backbone of the traditional academic reward system. When given in recognition of significant professional accomplishment, rewards provide powerful, well-spaced incentives. If used well with effective annual evaluation and salary adjustments, few other incentives may be needed. If not used well, other forms of faculty incentives cannot compensate for these lost opportunities to encourage faculty professional growth.

Regular time for creativity and innovation is a precious intangible commodity. Release time, which allows the faculty to reset day-to-day priorities, deserves special attention as an incentive. In order to create time for the development of a new course or to finish a research project, it is often necessary to break the monotony of the regular schedule. At the University of Richmond, a faculty member may apply for release time from one or more courses for research, artistic work, teaching innovation, or course development. Release time provides a strong incentive for faculty members with worthwhile projects but insufficient time to accomplish them. The dean administers the allotment of release time each semester, and thus, accountability is easily maintained. The university regularly budgets for this program and hires part-time adjunct instructors. When such programs cannot be budgeted, other approaches are possible. For example, at the College of William and Mary, some larger departments create internal, unfunded sabbaticals or release time by absorbing the extra students in other sections of courses taught by departmental colleagues. This approach works well in larger departments and when there is strong group support for the process. Blocks of time for special projects can also be freed by creative scheduling. Mornings and alternate days free from classes can be arranged by cooperative department chairs and deans. This approach requires clear accountability and strong administration to prevent abuse.

The benefit of faculty workshops is obvious. The more timely the topic is and the more strongly the need is felt, the better the response from the faculty. In recent years such topics as the internationalization of the curriculum, the role of women and blacks in history and literature, and an introduction to computers have been used on many campuses to stimulate new thinking and perspectives on our teaching. Such programs bring together campus colleagues from different disciplines to learn from each other or from an outside expert about topics of broad interest. Another example illustrates this last point.

A broad understanding of the brain was the goal of an informal faculty summer seminar held at the University of Richmond. The seminar was organized around the topic of modern brain research and what it tells us about styles of learning and, therefore, about styles of teaching. This was not a workshop on teaching tips. Its goals were to inform the participants about a rapidly growing understanding of the human brain and the reasons, in terms of brain functions, why some styles of teaching lead to effective learning in some people but not in others. Twenty individuals from a wide spectrum of disciplines, from music to math to modern languages, were selected to participate because they represented different channels of learning. Movies, video-tapes, audio-tapes, a brain dissection, and a good reading list supplemented on-campus faculty expertise in psychology, brain physiology, and education.

If faculty members are motivated, as I believe we are, by a desire for respect and recognition of our knowledge and expertise, powerful incentives arise from giving us responsibility or authority in areas of our interest and expertise. Naturally, these incentives come into play when we give the faculty primacy over curriculum matters, graduation requirements, and the like. Yet we rarely recognize lesser examples of empowering individuals or small groups of faculty for what they are: opportunities for faculty creativity and excitement. Whether to organize and run seminars, conferences, special curriculums, or other programs, we are all more motivated when it is our project. The more we can recognize and support opportunities for the faculty members to exercise authority (and responsibility), the more they are likely to respond with genuine commitment. Sometimes we hesitate to empower out of concern that the individual will feel overwhelmed by the project, or worse, that the project might not be run the way we want it run. Careful negotiation before and during the project, with clear expectations and criteria for assessment may relieve some concern. The remaining risk may be worth the positive results it can produce.

One final observation about direct and intangible incentives: Recognition of good work is important for everyone—faculty members included. Recognition in campus publications, at campus events, and in informal but public interaction helps to reinforce what we value and think is important. When praise is sincere and deserved, it cannot be overdone.

Indirect and Tangible. Less obvious motivators of the faculty are the indirect but tangible incentives generated by good facilities, equipment, and libraries. They are part of the quality of the work environment that reinforces the perception of faculty value and esteem. A good and supportive teaching and research environment encourages good work. An unsupportive environment discourages good work.

Of special value to the atmosphere of teaching and research is the faculty club, a place where the faculty can conduct business in a social but professional setting. Faculty morale, self-esteem, and receptiveness to professional development programs can be higher, all other things being equal, when faculty members have a place of their own.

Indirect and Intangible. The last group of incentives is the most difficult to assess directly and the most often overlooked. But these incentives are nevertheless important as effective motivators when the goal is a creative, productive, and proud faculty. Although they satisfy few of the ten keys described above, they are the spice of our intellectual lives. Only a few examples of indirect and intangible incentives are given here, but numerous others can be found if considered from the right perspective.

The first of these is a regular forum for the faculty to present to colleagues reports on their scholarly projects. In its most positive role, such forums allow the speakers to share their ideas with others and to benefit from others' questions and perspectives. The audience of peers may gain new respect for the kind of intellectual work done by colleagues. These interactions from time to time result in new teaching or scholarly collaborations that may also lead to new vitality. Because of the isolation created by our departmental structure and highly specialized research, a faculty forum is also an effective way to increase faculty intellectual interaction and just to get faculty members acquainted with each other. By asking individuals returning from sabbatical leaves to give presentations on their scholarly projects, I have also found the forum-among-one's-peers to be a good way to hold individuals accountable for the productive use of sabbatical time. The main value of an intellectual forum among peers is that it helps to build pride and a true sense of belonging to a community of scholars. Obviously, this is a major motivator of our best faculty members. (A word about attendance. Measure success realistically. A few regulars will attend every event, some will attend now and then, others will never attend. If 10 to 20 percent of the faculty members attend, count the event a success. Schedule the event in a room too small for the number expected to show up.)

We all recognize the insularity of our institutions and the importance of bringing in new ideas and perspectives. We host a variety of outside speakers on our campuses each year to break the isolation. Their role is to stimulate and inform us. We also invite visitors to fill in for faculty on leave or to fill unexpected vacancies. In hiring our visiting professors, we often focus on covering the courses and under-utilize these opportunities for faculty development. We rarely ask what the visitor can teach the faculty, or what role the visitor can play in faculty development. A deviation from this pattern may be created by special visiting professorships in which one of the obligations is to offer a course for the faculty. Such was the case at William and Mary in 1985 when a distinguished visiting professor in humanities taught a provocative semester-long seminar, which forty faculty members attended. Intuitively, the short-range benefits were positive and broadly felt. The long-range benefits are still unfolding.

Similarly, the opportunities for our faculty members to serve as visiting professors at other institutions are under-utilized. Because many faculty members have dual-career families, children in school, and other obligations, it may be difficult for them to arrange to be away for a semester or a year, but the rewards are worth the effort. A cost-efficient way of allowing faculty members to serve as visiting members of another institutions' faculty is to exchange faculty members for a year. If each institution pays its own faculty member's salary, there is little cost to the program. However, moving and other expenses are incurred and deserve institutional support if faculty members are to feel encouraged to participate. The League of Institutions for Faculty Exchange (LIFE), run by Trinity University, organizes and coordinates exchanges of this sort for a group of institutions, including the

University of Richmond. The Center for Faculty Exchange is a broader program coordinated at Franklin and Marshall College.

Finally, among the best incentives are intellectually active and productive colleagues and bright and challenging students. Incentive programs cannot create these incentives, they can only help them achieve their potential.

Zeddie Bowen is vice-president and provost of the University of Richmond, in Richmond, Virginia.

The chair, the dean or provost, and the director of faculty development can most easily guide and monitor the effective delivery of incentives.

Who Has the Role of Building in Incentives?

John M. Bevan

I was sitting across the table from the wife of a professional friend who had decided, after spending fifteen years in teaching and research at the university, to accept an industrial position. With pronounced glee, she told me about the joy her husband and several of his new colleagues had experienced recently when they were recognized for their accomplishments at a banquet given in their honor. They had developed a sensitive drug for the early detection of Acquired Immune Deficiency Syndrome (AIDS). Top management had arranged for a seven-course dinner, at which each researcher was toasted and presented with an especially designed sterling silver lapel button. "My husband came away feeling like the celebrity he is, proud of himself for what he and his colleagues have done, aware that the people upstairs knew he had made a contribution to the advancement of science and the betterment of society." She added that her husband had spent many years at the university, published dozens of articles, participated on more committees than he had had time for, worked hard at being an effective teacher, presented papers at meetings in this country and abroad, and brought in grants in sufficient sums that the indirect costs paid his and his co-workers' salaries. Never once, however, had anyone said, "Thanks"; never once had the president or a dean or his department chair suggested to him

R. G. Baldwin (Ed.). *Incentives for Faculty Vitality.* New Directions for
Higher Education, no. 51. San Francisco: Jossey-Bass, September 1985.

that he was doing a good job. Why? Now, she said, he feels enthusiastic and every morning leaves the house anxious to repeat the successes he has had during the past year. "I'll tell you, universities in this country are riding for a big fall. It's no wonder industries want to produce their own Ph.D.s." The attitudes engendered in the university frustrate and depress, rather than challenge and encourage. The woman ended by saying, "One thing I know, what is taking place in my husband's life now has given him a new sense of worth and renewed vigor that will propel him for years."

Later that evening, as I reflected on this conversation, I wondered if our universities might be destined for the same fate as today's U.S. coal, steel, shoe, and textile industries. One thought led to another. I recalled a colleague contending that colleges and universities are basically normative organizations and that individual commitment to the organization, if such commitment exists, results from the intrinsic value of the enterprise rather than the extrinsic rewards associated with membership. He (Sagen, 1972) made the following conclusions:

1. Faculty norms at most institutions emphasize allegiance to a specific discipline and to education as the transmission of subject matter.

2. The norms assume that faculty members are independent professionals who contract with the institution for their services.

3. Faculty members prefer a collegial or consensual mode of decision making that respects the domain of each faculty member and his or her academic area.

4. The norms are enforced through faculty prestige granted by colleagues who share these norms and through a reward system that is usually controlled by senior faculty members or their administrative representatives.

Of course, shared norms, values, and attitudes in such a complex setting, increasingly bureaucratic and competitive, are something else. Wise (1968, p. 49) states, "Most college faculties are almost totally unprepared to participate in thoughtful consideration of educational policy and institutional purposes." So much for the conclusion that the viability, vitality, and achievement of these organizations depend on the personal commitment of every participant to the circumstances that ensure the greatest growth and self-fulfillment for each member of the organization. Debates on work load, on criteria for promotion and tenure, and on the number of credit hours required to complete the major take precedence in academic forums over debate on curriculum, mission, and social responsibility because of the fact that everyone is capable of debating procedure but few are ready to debate the meaning or philosophical foundations of the very institutions they serve. No wonder a faculty seldom revises its curriculum by means other than a band-aid approach.

Fortunately, there are occasions when the interaction between faculty members focuses on humanistic involvement in academe. I will never forget the young associate professor who walked into my office after hearing me refer to the faculty as a "resource pool" and challenged me to make it possible for her to serve as a resource person for her colleagues. She had a Ph.D. in art history, with an excellent background in history, psychology, mathematics, and science. She was a resource person and she was ready to entertain invitations from colleagues to lecture in those courses in which her expertise might add further illumination. After some maneuvering of schedules and hours, she was given funding for the summer and a one-course-load reduction for both of the next two semesters to become the college's first in-house visiting lecturer. Colleagues responded immediately to her appeal with such topic requests as "Scientific Concepts of the Modern World as Reflected in Art" (Introduction to Biology), "Man's Visualization of His Gods" (History of Religion), "Interaction of Mind-Eye Patterns" (General Psychology), "Transformation of Medieval to Renaissance as Seen in Visual Art" (History of Western Europe), "Concepts of Baroque Style" (Baroque Music).

Invitations to lecture were always followed by a conversation with the regular professor to determine the objectives of the presentation; evaluation conversations were held after the lectures, frequently followed by requests for additional lectures. In all, she made twenty-seven guest lectures that year, with great satisfaction derived by both participating colleagues and the lecturer. Such an appointment, regarded as prestigious and subsequently held by others, stressed the importance and the expansive worth of faculty members, and it supported a dynamic and integrative structure of development—a dialogue spanning the intellectual community, including literature, history, mathematics, science, philosophy, theology, the arts, and social sciences.

In this context of faculty as a resource pool (Bevan, 1978), the character and uniqueness of any college is not left to specific disciplines, but to the interaction between persons of differing disciplines within the institution. The validity of the community rests on what can and does happen when academicians interact, recognizing that what happens, then, happens because of the real expertise of those in a given field and not in spite of their expertise. In such a setting there may be as many programs as there are human beings, each program contributing distinctiveness. The idea of a pool of resource persons provides an almost limitless number of programming options within a given institution, certainly as many combinations as there are persons. This same resource pool, if open, can draw on other resources such as career service interns, adjunct faculty, community experts, visiting scholars, and artists. The interactions ensure not only a dynamic diversity but also the continuous interdisciplinary discourse necessary for a common language and critical to developing values, standards, and skills of discrimination. In such settings faculty members come together to talk about educational and intellectual rather than disciplinary and bureaucratic matters. Furthermore, what emerges, I believe, is an education for enlightened self-interest. Ideas that stand the test of debate and are appreciated, scholarly exchanges of agreement and disagreement in one's own and in other fields, the sense of contribution to a dialogue that has meaning beyond oneself and engages one with others in what is most important to and needed by oneself and others—these are what binds all those in intellectual pursuits and brings the rewards and vitality most characteristic of the profession, regardless of discipline.

A resource pool concept commends the distinctiveness of and expertise in various disciplines while depending on interaction between the differing disciplines to maintain an intellectually vigorous community. We have a responsibility to provide in academe a structure and a way of life that reinforces community and maintains and enhances the autonomy and power of the parties so critical to the enterprise. And if we think in terms of an educational community, then it is important that we deal in a style befitting an educational model, that is, one that espouses openness, not secrecy; truth and understanding, not misinformation; trust, not suspicion; full participation, not minimal compliance; the use of conflict for creative cooperation, not for control and spoils; the sharing of power by all parties, not an imbalance of power. In an academic community where such an attitude as this prevails, we might talk enthusiastically about the greatest growth and self-fulfillment for the majority.

Who can best apply incentives to foster faculty vitality? Who can manipulate most easily the existing institutional structure and its operating systems to deliver effective incentive programs and create the dynamic setting required to bolster morale? Primarily three persons: the department chair, the dean or provost, and the director of faculty development.

The Department Chair

It is most unsettling to find oneself flung suddenly into the fray, where tough questions are raised daily and decisions expected on faculty evaluation, faculty recruitment, faculty raises, faculty morale, faculty feuds, faculty tenure and promotion, midlife and midcareer changes, the funding of program development, legal rights of the administration and of colleagues, departmental and institutional goals couched in planning and more planning, and so on; and where maintaining and enhancing the posture of the department within the college or university is essential to being considered a successful leader. Of course, the one who serves as leader may be regarded as effective because he or she is efficient at overseeing the repair of typewriters, the replenishing of supplies, the punctual distributing of memos, the securing of additional secretarial help, or a little more travel money, and never strays from what faculty consensus dictates on all matters both large and small. But whatever the case, the department chair's principal responsibilities are to develop effective professors, to maintain and enhance effective professors, and to reward effective professors whose behavior is effective because it reinforces the good image of the profession and the university through the attainment of the goals of the department and the institution.

What is the successful department chair like, and how does he or she create a setting supportive of faculty vitality? There is no stereotype (Bevan, 1982). Such a person may be formal or informal but is accessible and relaxed when talking with a colleague. Even when anxious, the chair should maintain an "at ease" appearance. While with colleagues, attention should be focused on what colleagues have to say, interacting in conversation by expanding on their ideas, analyzing their problems, suggesting outcomes, expressing excitement when an idea strikes a spark, always cautious not to hold out false promises, and avoiding the easy reply that a problem is beyond the range of the chair's authority. Furthermore, because the department chair should avoid being strapped to a desk, he or she may often be found in a departmental colleague's office, talking about an article or paper the colleague has published on presented, enjoying an exchange on a subject near and dear to the colleague's heart, sharing some information about a possible source of funding for a research project the colleague mentioned a short while back, or passing on a compliment some student made about the colleague's classroom effectiveness. Or the department chair may be there to brief a new assistant professor on protocol, because as much as anyone in the department the chair realizes that young faculty members are only beginning the career-long process of becoming fully competent professional teachers, advisers, evaluators, committee workers, educational philosophers, and researchers who need skills that should be acquired through training and not through a haphazard process of socialization. Also, the department chair should be a sensitive leader, cognizant of the pressures provoked by the competition for tenure. I will never forget meeting one young faculty member shortly after a brief encounter with the department chair. He was struggling to hold back tears when I unexpectedly came upon him. For two weeks he had been anxiously waiting to hear about his tenure decision. In the hallway upstairs he had just met his department chair, who, avoiding his glance, greeted him by saying, "The committee didn't grant you tenure, but let's discuss it later when I have time." Numbed, this young man could only nod.

For an hour and a half each year, the department chair sits down with each department colleague to review systematically his or her performance and to talk about what the future holds for that person, that is, what the department's goals are and what role the professor plays in its growth. It is a candid conversation held privately with tenured and nontenured faculty members. This is a regularly scheduled session set up to guarantee a colleague knowledge about his or her professional standing, and at the same time, to learn how and what that colleague is thinking. An intellectual

community, such as an academic department, cannot grow and be productive if its leader does not know how and what each member thinks. The
leader's evaluation of a faculty member must likewise be known to that
individual. More than any other responsibility, these interviews are critical to
establishing a level of expectancy, quality, cohesiveness, and camaraderie.
Yet this very important process tends to be avoided by chairs of departments
and faculty members alike. Why is it so difficult to talk about such matters as
the quality of the teaching materials used, the intellectual tasks set for the
students, the results of student ratings, effective teaching and learning styles,
the responsibilities related to the department's mission, scholarly activities
and productivity, the interaction between the faculty and students, or
exchanges with colleagues outside the department and the college? Uninter-
rupted moments such as these are to be affirmed and remembered, as are
moments set aside to discuss what a colleague thinks and does, what the
colleague regards as vital to his or her professional and personal life, what the
colleague excels in and where improvement should be pursued, and whether
new options should be tried or familiar ones embraced.

The colleagues of a supportive department chair know they are
accepted and appreciated because members of the department are
nominated for institutional awards, such as research and teaching awards;
because their schedules are rearranged to permit load reductions for writing
and participating in interdisciplinary seminars; because they are encouraged
to apply for summer study abroad seminars or internships arranged by the
college through the United States Information Agency or the U.S.
Department of Education; or because sabbaticals are discussed and
encouraged. Also, colleagues feel confidently represented in the court of the
institution because they feel well served by a leader who balances their needs
aggressively and fairly with the needs of their department, of other
departments, and of the university or college as a whole. Department
members in such a setting sense cohesive feeling of movement, pride,
enthusiasm, and enlightened self-interest.

The Dean

The person who should know better than anyone else where the
institution is going (in fact, had better know) is the academic dean. Also, he or
she had better know how to keep the vision alive, particularly when that
means realignment or renewal. The dean should design and maintain a
climate for the students that is deliberate, taxing, dynamic, and anxiety-
provoking, and that at the same time fosters excitement, involvement, and a
profound impact of the professor in learning. As the program emerges, new
forms and meanings take shape, and the dean must expedite delivery and
nurture development. The dean's instruments are long-range planning,

good timing, good counseling, and an understanding and appreciation of academic governance. The total scheme and strategy may be known only to the dean, and each phase revealed only when the community has been readied. The dean may move in one instance with radical speed and in another with delayed precision. Continually, and almost always with the assistance of the department chairs, the dean systematically and informally evaluates the people in relation to the program and the program in relation to the people and both in relation to the objectives. Of course, if the dean spends a lot of time shuffling paper or running from one committee meeting to the next, he or she could be displaced from the center of activity, become ineffective in gauging dynamics and quality, and rather quickly could become a dogmatic potentate or a proliferous messenger of proleptic memos. In this role, the dean may keep the boat from tipping but would no longer be an abrasive agent of creative disequilibrium.

After making an analysis of the students and coming to a grasp of the aims of education and the mission of the institution, the dean must define (or provoke a definition of) the major development he or she wants to see made in the students, mastermind an academic vehicle for its expression, and serve as a catalyst and engineer in its realization. It is fine if the dean has ideas, but it is much more important that he or she possess and exercise the critical ability to select from among the most promising ideas. Then, along with the best faculty members, the dean should work out a program that exploits judiciously everyone's highest potential. The faculty establishes the tone and tempo of an institution of higher learning, and because the most important component of academe is the faculty, the dean's most important responsibilities are the recruiting of faculty, the evaluating of faculty, and the maintaining and enhancing of faculty (Bevan, 1967).

In recruitment the dean must depend on the chairs of the departments but does not leave the decision solely to the chair. The objectives of the institution and its program demand characteristics often extending beyond the range of the department itself. The dean searches for scholars who have depth and command in their fields of specialization, yet possess enough breadth of cultural background to relate their own field of study to the totality of experience; who demonstrate personal and professional growth through involvement in research, publication, and other professional activities; who inspire in students a respect for their profession; who possess the ability to make students think and act independently, creatively, and with maximum vigor; who extend themselves to their students in service, to their colleagues in cooperation, and to their community in concern; and whose character the students will want to emulate.

But the dean does not leave evaluation to department chairs alone. There is no means of satisfactorily managing the learning process without regular assessment of the key instruments. Every faculty member, regardless of tenure, should be subjected annually to a critique of his or her performance. The dean must expedite this process, even if it takes the assistance of a dictum from the president or the trustees.

Director for Faculty Development

This person is the broker, the negotiator of contracts of various types, and the identifier and coordinator of resources, both human and material. He or she moves about campus gathering information for requests or projects that may apply immediately or at some later date. The request may come from any one of many sources, such as the dean or provost; a library of annual foundation reports and its corresponding directory of names and telephone numbers; the faculty development committee, the faculty research committee, or the faculty development and research committee; a budgeted amount of money provided to seed projects (until enough data are available to justify writing a proposal for larger, outside grants); or the department chairs, with whom group meetings are held several times each year. The director for faculty development is more than a vital communications link. His or her office services degree completion, supports new course planning, fosters instructional improvement using new audio-video and computer techniques, supervises the awarding of mini-grants, arranges professional growth contracts, schedules and plans faculty retreats and skills workshops on the order of competency learning and self-pacing, provides opportunities for mentor training and career options counseling, encourages sabbatical leaves and administrative internships, and even introduces pertinent reading materials into the faculty lounge.

It is surprising how much conversation between persons of differing disciplines can be generated by this designated broker and his or her appointed or elected committees, particularly when there is easy access to the dean and the department chairs. For instance, it did not take long to find out how many people on campus were interested in publishing book-length manuscripts but did not know how to make the necessary arrangements. Once this fact was established, little effort or ingenuity was needed to arrange a two-day campus visitation by a few university press and commercial press editors for meetings with the prospective authors, in groups and individually. The first time I attended such a gathering, thirty-five faculty members responded enthusiastically to four editors. About eighteen months later, six books had been published, all of which were the first books to be published by these authors, who had informally reinforced each other during this generative period.

What a wonderful protagonist the director of faculty development can be for faculty members in such situations as the classics Ph.D. of ten years who has never been to Greece and is seeking some financial assistance so that he might see the places he refers to frequently in class; or for the recent retiree with whom a few students wish to study independently; or for the young art historian interested particularly in the works of Frank Lloyd Wright, yet who has seen very few of Wright's major contributions; or for the ABD instructor who wants to complete her dissertation but finds it impossible to teach four courses a term, do research, and write; or for the professor who wishes to improve her instructional effectiveness but does not have the $2,000 necessary for equipment and secretarial aid to prepare extra materials; or for the colleague who has completed a very significant paper but does not have the necessary funding to attend the professional meeting at which the paper should be presented; or for so many others with different and similar requests who are being encouraged and are anxious to improve themselves as teachers, scholars, and resourceful citizens.

The director of faculty development, the dean, and a few responsive department chairs working cooperatively and openly can create an atmosphere that will develop faculty members in the profession, keep the profession growing and strongly competitive, and attract strong persons to the profession. Admittedly, what is called for is more than the traditional format of faculty development, that is, support for research, funding to attend professional meetings, and the occasional half-year sabbatical with full pay or the full-year sabbatical with half pay. Nor does faculty vitality permeate an academic community as a result of isolated events centered around a few persons. A handful of outstanding scholars can contribute significantly, but seldom do they constitute the critical mass necessary to create a dynamic setting for productive interaction that grips the community and makes it an exciting place to be, a place where interactions ensure not only a dynamic diversity but also the continuous interdisciplinary discourse critical to developing personal values and skills necessary for refining humanistic experience and sustaining the kind of vibrant academic outreach critical to enhancing society.

In maintaining and enhancing the academic vitality of a campus, there are conditions and strategies that facilitate or inhibit development (Smith, 1976). These will vary, of course, according to the strength of leadership, size, location, financial resources, faculty resources, and ways in which the faculty perceives itself. A concise sample listing of these factors follows.

Key Factors That Facilitate Vitality

1. *Decisive leadership and support.* The critical element is coordinated administrative and faculty leadership that is committed to cooperation. This means inclusive as well as incisive leadership, giving a leader the opportunity to advocate his or her personal choices in a setting that gives an equal voice and hearing to any opposing point of view.

2. *An informal academic posture.* Such an environment relies heavily on personal interaction, on incidental hallway and sidewalk conversations as possible times for conducting official negotiations, and on administrators who circulate.

3. *A common understanding of mission and corresponding professional expectations.* Different corporate cultures cultivate different values and loyalties. How different would be the conduct of one's life as a chemist working in a liberal arts setting as compared to one's life as a chemist in an industrial setting.

4. *Attention to new faculty.* Not knowing how to perform well prevents career satisfaction. Young academicians are only beginning the career-long process of becoming professional teachers, mentors, researchers, and authors.

5. *Attention to mature faculty.* Not keeping up prevents career satisfaction and affects morale negatively. Senior members are engaged in an unending process of retooling, recharging, refining, and extending professional and personal development.

6. *Rewards correlated with talent.* Research time is granted for excelling in research, teaching preparation time for excelling in teaching, writing time or travel time for those who author books and exhibit works of art, perform, and lecture.

7. *Salary increments reflect merit effort and accomplishment primarily.* Assessment is the handmaiden of development and is conducted in a tactfully straightforward manner . . . in the quest of self actualization.

8. *Monies budgeted for faculty development.* Because faculty members are a college's or university's primary resource for stimulating learning and are the central force in maintaining and enhancing its character, vitality and outreach, at least 1 percent of the sum spent annually for academic operation should be designated to this end.

9. *Academic structure and program regarded as malleable.* The curriculum as defined in the catalogue and scheduled by the registrar does not control faculty each semester; the faculty and its leaders control the curriculum. Adaptations in course and faculty scheduling can be made to meet faculty members' needs when such changes do not violate the integrity of the program or impede a student's progress.

10. *Good timing, sensitive and flexible planning.* To know if and when a consensus has been reached is a vital part of the scheme of transaction . . . using a range of strategies that include individuals, small groups, forums, and seed monies.

11. *Training academic managers to employ incentives effectively.* As stated earlier, new skills and expertise in this area are acquired by the process of socialization, not training. The dean and director of faculty development should be able to contribute significantly to such learning.

Key Factors That Inhibit Vitality

1. *Insulated departments.* This is less likely in the smaller institution, but common in the large university. Structural factors usually contribute to insulation; vitality and support are centered in research, exchange with colleagues of other departments is happenstance, and a faculty resource pool concept with its interdisciplinary perspective is seldom part of such a department's projections.

2. *Competitive and turf control posture.* Dominance of departmental structures results in fragmented goals and objectives, heightens competition for limited resources, and also results in unnecessary duplication. Cooperation is possible only after the question of control is settled—hardly a satisfactory attitude for inspiring joint undertakings.

3. *Limited options for continuing development.* Work load does not permit time for professional experimentation, nor are opportunities available for on-campus leadership. Continuing development is not considered a continuing incentive.

4. *An excessive number of innovative ventures.* Too many projects undertaken in a narrow band of time may produce suppressive faculty work loads, confusion of ideas, frustration, and exhaustion. Over-indulging in community projects in some cases has also threatened the internal integrity of a college's program.

5. *False promises.* When reality does not come up to intended expectations, anger and resentment spill over, and involvement is curtailed. A breach of trust stifles interest in taking advantage of future suggestions and opportunities.

6. *Poor communication.* Lack of information provokes charges of not being consulted or of being manipulated, resulting in failure to enlist sufficient faculty and administrative support.

7. *No correlation between faculty development and student development goals.* Frequent mismatches will discourage participation (for example, faculty travel abroad opportunities but no programs for students to study abroad, or opportunities for faculty in research but no arrangements for students to gain credit for the design and completion of certain of their own academic pursuits).

8. *The threat of open assessment.* Faculty members mastering new techniques or pursuing new instructional approaches and attaining knowledge may mean exposing one's inadequacies to others, as in the case of avoiding computer literacy workshops.

This list might be extended, but few surprises would be revealed. Even if we analyzed each condition cited, little in the way of added illumination would be derived. Furthermore, a condition in evidence on one campus may represent something quite different on another campus. In all

56

likelihood, what is more interesting and meaningful are the signs of increased vitality.

Signs of Increased Vitality

Several signs characteristic of new vitality on campus are (1) new mixes, for example, more senior faculty with younger faculty, new interdisciplinary groups, more collaboration through research and seminars, more engagement of constituents outside the institution; (2) an increase and broader involvement of faculty members in the mainstream of college life, for example, cultural affairs, scholarly lectures and readings, formal functions for distinguished visitors, and student affairs; (3) increased faculty productivity and professional participation, for example, presentation of papers, publications, and attendance at professional meetings; (4) changes in the "style of opposition" to new efforts (more reflective and less emotional), an increase in the generation of new ideas, and the recognition of the new needs resulting from the infusion of new ideas; (5) changes in priorities and accompanying changes in operational policy and the allocation of resources; (6) heightened enthusiasm expressed by the faculty, students, and other groups for the future of the institution; and (7) an increased flow of energy into every aspect of institutional life.

Another important sign is the variety of awards available in a college or university setting. Somewhere our institutions have lost sight of the faculty as a group of very different individuals needing different kinds of incentives to stimulate and expand potential. Faculty development and faculty evaluation repeatedly substantiate this conclusion, yet the rewards offered in response are standard and rather sterile. New approaches to incentives must be explored, approaches that nourish and are productive of a dynamic academic milieu. New impetus may come merely by adding to the traditional rewards: in-house visiting lecturers, mini-grants, internal sabbaticals, after-tenure rewards, faculty-named scholarships, banking credits, student assistant grants, research resources fellows (Bevan, 1979).

References

Bevan, J. M. "The Deanship." *Liberal Education,* 1967, *13* (3), 3–13.

Bevan, J. M. "Faculty Resource Pool: Mark of an Innovative Institution." *North Carolina Libraries,* 1978, *35,* 33–41.

Bevan, J. M. "Faculty Evaluation and Instructional Rewards." In W. O'Connell, Jr. (Ed.), *Improving Undergraduate Education in the South.* Atlanta, Ga.: Southern Regional Education Board, 1979.

Bevan, J. M. "The Chairman: Product of Socialization or Training?" In G. French-Lazovik (Ed.), *Practices That Improve Teaching Evaluation.* New Directions for Teaching and Learning, no. 11. San Francisco: Jossey-Bass, 1982.

Sagen, H. B. "Organizational Reform Is Not Enough." In C. U. Walker (Ed.), *Elements Involved in Academic Change.* Washington, D.C.: American Association of Colleges, 1972.

Smith, H. E. "Renewing Liberal Arts Colleges: Report of the Project on the Assessment of Institutional Renewal." New Haven, Conn.: Society for Values in Higher Education, 1976.

Wise, W. M. *The Politics of the Private College.* New Haven, Conn.: The Hazen Foundation, 1968.

John M. Bevan is executive director of the Charleston Higher Education Consortium. He has also served as chief academic officer of Davidson College, in North Carolina; Florida Presbyterian (now Eckerd College); University of the Pacific, in California; and the College of Charleston, in South Carolina.

Intrapersonal needs that drive the development process can affect the person-environment fit, thus leading to changes in vitality.

Developmental Needs as Intrinsic Incentives

Janet H. Lawrence

College and university administrators are seeking ways to maintain the vitality of their most important resource—the faculty. In this chapter, present conditions within higher education are examined within the context of developmental theory, and policies and practices that may enhance the performance of professors are discussed.

Productivity and work satisfaction are functions of the "person-environment fit." Person-environment fit represents the congruence between the characteristics of individuals, their needs and abilities, and the "supplies and demands of environment as expressed in role expectations and prerequisites" (Kahn, 1979, p. 78). The "fit" can be improved by any combination of the following practices: (1) employing individuals whose abilities match the tasks required by the work role; (2) rewarding people who increase their ability to perform in response to changing environmental demands; and (3) supporting individuals as they pursue self-defined goals that may prove beneficial to the organization. In the first two instances, motivation is heightened by conditions that "pull" (Cummings and Schwab, 1973) individuals toward a particular behavior (extrinsic incentives). In the third case, needs that exist within a person (intrinsic incentives) "push" him to behave in ways that will satisfy those needs.

R. G. Baldwin (Ed.). *Incentives for Faculty Vitality.* New Directions for Higher Education, no. 51. San Francisco: Jossey-Bass, September 1985.

Baldwin (1979) has suggested that faculty vitality and institutional well-being can be enhanced by moving faculty members to different roles as their developmental needs (intrinsic incentives) change. Unfortunately, evidence from empirical studies does not support prescriptive applications of existing models of academic career stages. Researchers have, by and large, failed to verify the universality of the model stages or the needs subsumed within them (Lawrence and Blackburn, in press; Clark and others, 1984). However, common motivational themes (clusters of intrapersonal needs that are assumed to drive the development process) do appear in the adult and career development literature. The themes of control and search for meaning provide a useful framework for discussing development-related incentives that may affect the person-environment fit and faculty vitality.

Developmental Themes

Control of the Environment. Throughout our lives, we have a persistent need to alter our environment, so that we can achieve transient goals or, over time, make our social environment consistent with our values. The drive to control is a central theme in Guttman's (1973) theory of adult male development. He asserts that as men age, they go through a series of stages in which their primary orientation to the world shifts from active to passive to magical mastery. In the first stage, men try to control through domination. However, at some time during their middle years, men realize that they cannot always dominate but must control by means of compromise and negotiation (passive mastery). They must create arrangements they can live with, even though they may not be ideal. In their later years, men may become defensive in their orientation to the world, believing that others are to blame for their present situation and that they have little or no control (magical mastery).

Guttman places the greatest emphasis on control, but the theme is also present in the writings of other developmentalists. Levinson's (1978) model of the structure of life includes alternating periods of stability and transition or instability, times when we seek to control and bring into balance the various aspects of our life. Likewise, Erikson (1963) and those who have elaborated on adult stages have given attention to the issue of generativity, the need to have an impact on one's environment that becomes one's legacy. In Loevinger's model (1976), growth progresses from a stage of conformity, when an individual accedes to the authority of others to achieve his or her goals, to more advanced stages in which behavior is the result of negotiation and accommodation (conscientious, individualistic, and autonomous stages).

In the vocational literature, control of the work environment and one's career direction are central issues. Dalton's model (in Hayes, 1981) of career stages characterizes development in terms of movement from positions in which one is under the control of others to those in which one has authority for oneself to positions in which one is ultimately responsible for others. Kanter (1979) differentiates between people who perceive that they are "moving" and those who are "stuck" in their career or institutional structures. She concludes that movers will be more productive and have a higher morale.

Baldwin and Blackburn's model of faculty career development (1981) assumes people move through initial phases in which they are under the control of others (pre-tenure) to ones in which they take more active roles in changing their institution (early associate professor through late-career). Clark, Corcoran, and Lewis (1984) found that promotion-delayed professors were more likely to exhibit a decline in vitality. The importance of control is further underscored by research that shows that productive faculty members take an active stance with respect to their environments (Pelz and Andrews, 1976) and are most satisfied when they have autonomy, that is, the freedom to pursue self-defined goals (Clark and others, 1984). Hodgkinson (1974) notes the feelings of diminished control that older professors may experience as they realize that their range of career options may be narrowing.

Search for Meaning. The second intrinsic incentive is the need to believe that what one does is important and that one's life-style is self-fulfilling. In Levinson's (1978) conceptualization of the life structure, transition periods are times when life review and the search for meaning are particularly salient. Individuals are constantly questioning the meaning of their lives, but during these times, people are particularly inclined to contemplate whether their lives are really what they want them to be. In the Erikson model (1963), the issue of integrity is key to development in the middle and later years. Unless individuals believe their lives have meaning, they experience despair and low morale. During Loevinger's (1976) early stages of development, meaning is provided by others, but the process from the conformity stage forward is one of individualization.

Work is an integral part of self-concept. Lifton (1976) states: "What we call work is a uniquely important boundary between self-process and social vision. Perhaps for the first time in history very large numbers of men and women are beginning to demand harmony and meaning at that boundary; to demand a reasonable equation between work and (works)" (p. 142). People will generally seek to make their work more meaningful or compensate by making a greater personal investment in other aspects of their lives. Certain work roles are intrinsically rewarding (for example, teaching or practicing medicine) and people who perform them are more ego-involved in their work (Kahn, 1979). Veroff, Douvan, and Kulka (1981) found that concern about the intrinsic value and meaning of work was particularly strong in college-educated persons. They tended to be more "ego-involved in what they experienced as satisfactions and dissatisfactions" (p. 9).

During the early phases of the academic career, activities are quite prescribed—at first by graduate faculty members and then by the tenure requirements of the institution (Blackburn, 1979). After achieving tenure, however, the need to find meaning, which may have been lying dormant, becomes a dominant force in a professor's career development (Braskamp and others, 1982). A faculty member strives toward a balance of life roles and professional activities so that his or her academic role has integrity. During the later phases of an academic career, a professor may be inclined to seek further consolidation of work roles and professional identity (Baldwin, 1979).

Locke, Fitzpatrick and White (1983) conclude that professors and employees in other types of organizations want many of the same things from their work: role clarity, a sense of achievement, and challenging work. The search for meaning may, however, lead to a redefinition of what challenging work is. Professors consistently give high ratings to the social significance of their work and the opportunities for stimulating intellectual interactions with colleagues and students. Pelz and Andrews (1976) suggest, however, that there may be age-related differences in intellectual interests. Preferences for divergent thinking and basic research seem to predominate in the early-career phases. Senior professors are more inclined toward convergent intellectual tasks and may be more interested in their roles as teachers.

Person-Environment Fit

Having described the developmental themes, I turn now to the question of person-environment fit. Are there instances when professors' inherent tendencies to search for meaning and control (intrinsic incentives) enhance the well-being of their colleges or universities? The overall conclusion is yes, but it is helpful to distinguish between those instances when all members of the institution benefit and those instances in which people experiencing certain career turning points might benefit most.

Points of Mutual Concern. The gradual professionalization of the academic role led to increasing specialization and faculty members came to hold memberships in two reference groups, each with its own set of norms. Disciplinary associations that were organized across campuses based their evaluations almost exclusively on contributions within the scholarly domain. The local faculty groups gave varying emphasis to performance as a teacher and performance as a researcher (Parsons and Platt, 1973).

In the mid to late 1970s, faculty members began to express their concern about the role-fragmentation and conflict they were experiencing. In a report on a 1977 faculty survey, Ladd (1979) wrote:

> A model is ascendant in academe, positing what faculty *should be doing,* that is seriously out of touch with what they *actually do* and *want to do.* The model is as well profoundly at odds with the primary goal of promoting the best possible teaching—that is the best educational

experience—in the nation's colleges and universities. . . . Can one think of a neater prescription for *malperformance:* Nurturing the claims among professors of a research model even though large majorities of them prefer teaching and are required by the concrete demands of their job to concentrate on teaching, combining so as to produce a diminished commitment to quality teaching and the substantial production of inferior research [pp. 6 and 7].

Peters and Waterman (1982) found that in the most successful corporations, a strong set of core values provided a framework within which central direction and individual autonomy could coexist. Hence, a key intersection exists between the personal needs of academicians to examine the meaning of their profession, and the obligation of the institution to "clarify what is central for the health, growth, and quality of the organization" (Keller, 1983, p. 75).

Professors are likely to have high ego investment in their work, and if their work has lost meaning for them, morale is likely to be low. Therefore, efforts to enhance vitality should include intellectually challenging discussions of the ideational base of the academic role. The focus must be on philosophical and ethical issues, the core values, rather than on the exigency conditions that have tended to frame most current debates. Perhaps open discussions of this sort will satisfy some of the genuine faculty needs that Brookes and German (1983) believe are not being met by current faculty development programs.

The second point of overlap is closely related to the first, but it derives from the intrinsic incentive to control. By nature and training, productive faculty members are inclined to take an active role in shaping their environments. The people in charge of the structure (administrators) and those responsible for implementing the mission (professors), cannot be at odds over their college's central purpose. Faculty members, by and large, do not want to manage the institution, but they certainly have a pressing need, by virtue of their ego involvement in their work and their developmental need for control, to participate in the formulation of policy. Frustration and feelings of impotence may likely exist on both sides, but participative management can ameliorate some of the problem.

A third intersection may exist. Professors are seeking to integrate their life roles in order to establish a meaningful balance between them. Higher education is being pressed by society to reintegrate its teaching and research functions. Parsons and Platt (1973) contend that the integration process is not particularly disruptive to individuals because these activities are actually different forms of learning. For some faculty members the process of integrating their work roles may involve scholarly inquiry, not with the intent to publish but to enhance their understanding of the subject matter they teach. For others, the task may be to learn how to communicate better with students. The optimal normative climate should support both efforts.

The fourth shared concern derives from the need of faculty members to feel controlled movement within their career structures and the need of institutions to resolve personnel problems that have resulted from financial restrictions. This intrinsic drive is not confined to a particular career stage, although it may be qualitatively different. An untenured professor writes, "The most defeating aspect of all has been the sense that I am essentially dispensible" (Rice, n. d., p. 14). Another faculty member states, "Above all, I want to avoid the acceptance of my present position as permanent. . . . I am struggling against 'settling down,' . . . But given the present situation in academia [depressed], there may not be a ladder to climb" (Rice, n. d., p. 14). There is no ready solution to the immediate problem. If the intrinsic incentive is strong, however, it may lead to creative role restructuring and eventually to new career norms. Such experimentation ought to be supported and its impact on an institution carefully evaluated, for personnel policies may emerge that will contribute to institutional well-being.

Turning Points. Developmental theories can increase our under- standing of faculty behavior, but they must be used in conjunction with other information about the individual and his or her social context. With this caveat, I will offer suggestions about types of support that may be particularly appropriate for professors who have experienced certain critical events, changes in their career situations, that make them alter their usual strategies, for coping with day-to-day life. Such turning points result in change beyond the threshold that can be dealt with routinely (Atchley, 1975).

Pre-Tenure. Newly appointed assistant professors encounter at least two major turning points in a short period. Most likely, they have been taught as graduate students to value the academic profession more highly than any other career option, and in particular, its research dimension. The process of developing classes and demonstrating potential as scholars may lead to the first turning point—the realization that when the research emphasis is on publication, the two activities, teaching and scholarship, may compete for precious time. They will benefit most from support that helps them function effectively and efficiently.

Some junior professors will be denied tenure, not necessarily because of their ability but because of conditions outside their control. This results in a second turning point, when they must make critical decisions about their future. I concur with Claxton and Murrell (1984), who urge department chairs to be frank about the conditions affecting tenure decisions, so that such decisions are less devastating to the candidate. I would add, however, that graduate faculty have an obligation to move their students away from the "one life, one career imperative" (Sarason, 1977) and to encourage them to explore various career tracks.

The faculty member's intrinsic "push" for control will be strong but may be sublimated while he or she is working for tenure. This is not a healthy arrangement. It is in the academician's and the institution's long-term best interest to have decisions regarding distribution of effort emphasize accommodation, a negotiated balance between both sets of priorities (individual and institutional).

Tenure to Mid-Career. The tenure turning point may trigger some to feel doubts about whether the academic life is really what they want. This intrinsically motivated search ought to be encouraged, even at the risk of losing some key individuals. Vitality may decrease if productive faculty members feel "stuck." Furthermore, experimentation may result in new alliances within and outside the school that may be mutually beneficial to the individual and institution.

As they move to midcareer, professors may find it refreshing to have the opportunity to negotiate their work loads as their orientation to the world shifts. This practice encourages academicians to think about alternative ways to structure their roles and build on their experiences. Discussions give administrators the opportunity to explain their perceptions of the fit between the individual's skills and interests and needs of the institution. To be successful, however, the process of accommodation must be a positive challenge and not a matter of coercion. It is important that both professors and department chairs present more than one option and develop a final agreement from a set of proposals.

Mid- to Late-Career. Given the current information explosion, there is a reasonable chance that senior professors may experience the feeling of obsolescence. At the same time, they may believe that their work has lost some of its challenge, and the desire for difficult tasks may be heightened (Bray and Howard, 1983). Even the most enriched jobs, those with high skill variety and autonomy, become boring and routinized after a period of time (Hayes, 1981).

Both of these very different age-related concerns can create stress and affect productivity. Persons who feel overwhelmed (possibly by the prospect of redirecting their research into evolving areas) or under-utilized (possibly by the prospect of changing their scholarly focus to conform with the new emphasis of funding agencies on application rather than on theory) may exhibit the same resistance to incentives for change. Therefore, administrators must be clear about the source of behavior and not conclude that it is merely age-related resistance to change triggered by the developmental need to consolidate activities.

The career development literature suggests that support for interdisciplinary activities is a particularly attractive incentive. The Group for Human Development in Higher Education (1974) advocates the use of "colleague groups" to counteract the current professional emphasis on specialization and institutional organization around the disciplines. These colleague groups provide a chance for faculty members who do not have formal preparation in a particular discipline but do have a "lively curiosity about it and a commitment to work within it" to come together around common interests (p. 71). Given the age-related preference for convergent thinking, such arrangements may be appealing to professors at this time in their careers and will contribute to institutional reintegration efforts.

Pre-Retirement. The productive researchers will probably not slow down in the years immediately preceding retirement. They often maintain the momentum built up over the years and, like their counterparts in other occupations (doctors, lawyers, politicians), continue their work after the institutionally mandated retirement age.

For the majority of professors, however, there is probably a sense of anticipatory loss as they contemplate the end of a role that has been an integral part of their identity. Institutions must provide opportunities for professors to move gradually out of an institution where they may have spent forty years. Phased retirement undoubtedly eases the transition for some professors, as it gives them a subsidized period to begin transferring their ego investment and building new life structures. In addition, colleges and universities can provide more proactive support for persons who are seeking to extend their work lives by helping them to find positions in other organizations or by putting their expertise to good use intramurally.

Conclusions

This brief review of the developmental and personality literature serves to remind professionals in higher education that faculty careers are determined in part by internalized needs. Administrators ought to be sensitive to the developmental issues and direct professors' energies in ways that are mutually beneficial to the individuals and to the institution. Recent investigations of aging and productivity suggest, however, that both maturational processes and environmental factors must be taken into account when assesssing changes in faculty behavior. Hence, current studies are shifting from an exclusive focus on either the person or the environment to designs that systematically account for interactions over time between individual attributes and institutional conditions.

College and university administrators can profit from careful monitoring of changes in faculty ability, interests, and behavior. The interpretation of these data is enriched by our knowledge of adult development. As we come to understand how interactions between individual characteristics and environmental conditions affect performance throughout the working years, administrators will be in a better position to modify policies and practices.

References

Atchley, R. C. "The Life Course, Age-Grading, and Age-Linked Demands for Decision Making." In N. Datan and L. Ginsberg (Eds.), *Life-Span Developmental Psychology: Normative Life Crises.* New York: Academic Press, 1975.

Baldwin, R. *The Faculty Career Process: Continuity and Change.* Unpublished doctoral dissertation, University of Michigan, 1979.

Baldwin, R. G., and Blackburn, R. T. "The Academic Career as a Developmental Process: Implications for Higher Education." *Journal of Higher Education,* 1981, *52* (6), 598–614.

Blackburn, R. T. "Academic Careers: Patterns and Possibilities." *Current Issues in Higher Education,* 1979, *2,* 25–27.

Braskamp, L., Fowler, D., and Dry, J. "Faculty Development and Achievement: A Faculty's View." Paper presented at the annual meeting of the American Educational Research Association, New York, April 1982.

Bray, D., and Howard, A. "The AT & T Longitudinal Studies of Managers." In K. W. Schaie (Ed.), *Longitudinal Studies of Adult Psychological Development.* New York: Guilford, 1983.

Brookes, M., and German, K. *Meeting the Challenges: Developing Faculty Careers.* Washington, D.C.: Association for the Study of Higher Education, 1983.

Clark, S. M., Corcoran, M., and Lewis, D. R. "Critical Perspectives on Faculty Career Development with Implications for Differentiated Institutional Policies." Paper presented at the annual meeting of the American Educational Research Association, New Orleans, April 1984.

Claxton, C. S., and Murrell, P. H. "Developmental Theory as a Guide for Maintaining the Vitality of College Faculty." In C. M. N. Mehrotra (Ed.), *Teaching and Aging.* New Directions for Teaching and Learning, no. 19. San Francisco: Jossey-Bass, 1984.

Cummings, L., and Schwab, D. *Performance in Organizations: Determinants and Appraisals.* Glenview, Ill: Scott, Foresman, 1973.

Erikson, E. H. *Childhood and Society.* (2nd ed.) New York: Norton, 1963.

Group for Human Development in Higher Education. *Faculty Development in a Time of Retrenchment.* New Rochelle, N.Y.: Change Publications, 1974.

Guttman, D. *In the Country of Old Men.* Occasional Papers on Aging. Ann Arbor: Institute of Gerontology, University of Michigan-Wayne State University, 1973.

Hayes, J. "Over Forties in Professional, Managerial, and Administrative Work." In G. Cooper and D. Torrington (Eds.), *After Forty: The Time for Achievement?* Chichester, England: John Wiley and Sons, 1981.

Hodgkinson, H. L. "Adult Development: Implications for Faculty and Administrators." *Educational Record,* 1974, 55 (4), 163–274.

Kahn, R. L. "Aging and Social Support." In M. Riley (Ed.), *Aging from Birth to Death.* Boulder, Colo.: Westview Press, 1979.

Kanter, R. M. "Changing the Shape of Work: Reform in Academe." *Current Issues in Higher Education,* 1979, *1,* 3–9.

Kanter, R. M. *The Change Masters: Innovations for Productivity in the American Corporation.* New York: Simon and Schuster, 1983.

Keller, G. *Academic Strategy: The Management Revolution in American Higher Education.* Baltimore, Md.: Johns Hopkins University Press, 1983.

Ladd, E. C., Jr. "The Work Experience of American College Professors: Some Data and an Argument." Paper presented at the National Conference on Higher Education sponsored by the American Association for Higher Education, Washington, D.C., 1979.

Lawrence, J., and Blackburn, R. "Faculty Careers: Maturation, Socialization, and Historical Effects." *Research in Higher Education,* in press.

Levinson, D., Darrow, C., Klein, E., Levinson, M., and McKee, B. *The Seasons of a Man's Life.* New York: Knopf, 1978.

Lifton, R. J. *The Life of the Self: Toward a New Psychology.* New York: Simon and Schuster, 1976.

Locke, E., Fitzpatrick, W., and White, F. "Job Satisfactions and Role Clarity Among University and College Faculty." *Review of Higher Education,* 1983, 6 (4), 343–365.

Loevinger, J. *Ego Development: Conceptions and Theories.* San Francisco: Jossey-Bass, 1976.

Parsons, T., and Platt, G. *The American University.* Cambridge, Mass.: Harvard University Press, 1973.

Pelz, D., and Andrews, F. *Scientists in Organizations.* Ann Arbor: Institute for Social Research, The University of Michigan, 1976.

Peters, T. J., and Waterman, R. H., Jr. *In Search of Excellence: Lessons from America's Best-Run Companies.* New York: Harper & Row, 1982.

Rice, R. E. *Dreams and Actualities: Danforth Fellows in Mid-Career.* Stockton, Calif.: University of the Pacific, n.d.

Sanford, N. "Academic Culture and the Teacher's Development." *Soundings,* 54 (4), 1971, 357–370.

Sarason, S. B. *Work, Aging, and Social Change: Professionals and the One Life-One Career Imperative.* New York: Free Press, 1977.

Veroff, J., Douvan, E., and Kulka, R. *The Inner American.* New York: Basic Books, 1981.

Janet H. Lawrence is associate professor in the Division of Higher, Adult and Continuing Education and is assistant research scientist at the Center for Research on Learning and Teaching at the University of Michigan. Her research focuses on the career development of college professors.

The institution, the disciplines, and the academic profession as a whole comprise a context that can enhance—or inhibit— vitality.

Faculty Vitality: The Professional Context

William Toombs

To the other chapters of this volume that consider incentives and motivation for the individual faculty member, this chapter adds a focus on aspects of the larger setting, the setting in which faculty efforts are interpreted. This is the milieu in which the fruits of incentives are met with endorsement and acceptance, or indifference, disbelief, rejection, and, occasionally, condemnation. Whatever heights faculty vitality may reach, these organizational factors can operate to check and frustrate good work.

Lament against the times, "O Tempora, O Mores," has a classic ring and academics themselves have a tradition of noble diatribe, perhaps best represented by the essays of Hutchins (1936) and Veblen (1918). Between the environment, which always contains anti-academic currents, and the individual faculty member is a boundary layer of special organizations. Our attention is directed to those boundary systems in which faculty members themselves have a great deal of influence if they choose to exercise it.

The academic profession, disciplines, and institutions have mediating, presentational, and interpretive functions with respect to larger society and its centers of power. They also operate as loci of membership and identity. Today the ability of such boundary-spanning units to translate and transmit the products of academic vitality is a matter of major importance. It

R. G. Baldwin (Ed.). *Incentives for Faculty Vitality.* New Directions for
Higher Education, no. 51. San Francisco: Jossey-Bass, September 1985.

speaks to the second definition of *vitality* in the Oxford English Dictionary: "The ability or capacity on the part of something of continuing to exist or to perform its function; the power of enduring or continuing." The root and branch of continuity reside with the profession at large, the disciplines, and the institutions.

An emphasis on boundary-spanning units, their organization, and their actions also fit well with two recent works. Within a little more than a year, two fine analyses of the American professoriate will have been published (Finkelstein, 1984; Bowen and Schuster, 1986). One contains a review of the profession's historical threads, including research findings. The other offers a full tapestry of the faculty landscape in the 1980s. In one sense a complete description of a given phenomenon stands as an explanation of many determinant factors in its existence. This is the taxonomic approach, illustrated by biology, wherein the description and arrangement of species and varieties fulfills the concepts of evolutionary theory. But there is an ecology to be studied as well: the relationships among "species" and between species and the environment. Znaniecki recognized the social implications of these two facets in his *Social Role of the Man of Knowledge* (1940), distinguishing one as composition and structure, and the other as behavior in the social order (Merton, 1973). The profession, the discipline, and the institution are in that latter boundary zone that influences behavior in the academic community.

The Profession

There is not the slightest doubt that the academics constitute a profession, and even have a claim as one of the learned professions, along with law, medicine, and theology. The work of college and university faculty in all dimensions meets the elementary criteria of a profession: foundations in theoretical knowledge, a body of skill in the use of that knowledge, and a requirement of wisdom in applying both knowledge and skill to particular circumstances (Goode, 1969; Anderson, 1974; Schein, 1972). The question of the degree to which academic work is an *established* profession is quite another matter.

Professions are acknowledged as social elites and accorded special status in society because they must engage serious issues, dangerous paradoxes, and areas of tenuous and fragmentary knowledge. For many decades the test of whether a field was "professional" depended on how many traits from a list of ideal components could be counted (Anderson, 1974; Hickson and Thomas, 1969).

A more dynamic conception emerges from the work of Hughes (1973), Vollmer and Mills (1966), Bucher and Strauss (1961), and the idea is well delineated by Houle (1981) as the process of professionalization. The critical information is no longer the mere presence or absence of attributes.

Neither does the number of attributes determine a position on some ideal scale of status. The principal factor is the degree to which the profession acts to move toward the goals of professionalism and the needs of the times. Houle consolidates much of the previous work into an action framework of characteristics of performance and collective identity toward which the professionalization process is directed. The criterion for judging a profession, professional vitality if you will, is how well the body of practitioners organizes itself and acts to improve the quality of practice.

We can examine professionalization with respect to the academic profession by using a set of criteria developed for the very practical purpose of deciding which professions could and should be involved in a long-term research and development project. The Continuing Professional Education Development Project at Penn State has worked for five years with teams for five professions: accounting, architecture, clinical dietetics, clinical psychology, and nursing (Smutz, 1981). The criteria, stated here as questions, by which these five professions were selected from a final panel of about fifteen provide an interesting lens through which to look at the academic profession.

1. Is there a coherent area of practice? Yes, the traditional trio of teaching, research, and service describes it.

2. Is there a good communication network? Yes, sound journals, good national meetings, and the *Chronicle of Higher Education* perform this function well.

3. Is the profession serving the public interest? Yes, but the exact and generally visible dimensions of that service are not well set in the public mind.

4. Is some form of permission to practice required? No, even worse, it is unheard of! Ladd and Lipset (1975) point out that the university has become the great legitimizing and certifying institution of contemporary societies.

5. Is there a well-developed organization representing the profession? No, and the absence stands as the most significant obstacle to sound professionalization and professional vitality. Houle (1981) observes that only those occupations whose members are deeply concerned with establishing their collective identities are considered "professions." Parsons and Platt (1968) emphasize that "institutionalized individualism" is the avenue by which professions attain recognition and freedom of practice. It is not the case that organizations are absent from the academic world. There are the American Council on Education (ACE), the American Association for Higher Education (AAHE), and the American Association of University Professors (AAUP), to mention the most comprehensive. Yet these are not true establishments of the profession. In the case of the ACE, it is a body of institutional representatives, not practitioners. The AAHE operates effectively as a forum but not as a policy body. The AAUP, which began in 1915 as

the seat of professional concerns, first failed to consolidate its strengths, for example, by electing to use censure instead of test cases in the public courts as the means of fixing the elements of professional behavior. In recent years decline has become a headlong descent demonstrated most recently in the Temple University case and captured in the words of the president of that institution, Peter Liacouras (1985, p. 18): "We deeply regret this attempt by the AAUP, the faculty labor union, to undermine the rule of law. . . . In our society the rule of law prevents the AAUP or anyone else from being a party to a case and also the judge, jury, and appellate court in deciding one's own case." Without a sound professional body, the claims and canons of the professional body are essentially unguarded. The historic consequences of that condition are amply demonstrated by the classic cases of encroachment on academic freedom, William Graham Sumner at Yale, Edward A. Ross at Stanford, Richard T. Ely at Wisconsin, Scott Nearing at Penn, and, by the general witch-hunting of the Palmer raids in the twenties and the McCarthy era.

6. Is there a recognizable path for continuing learning and professional development? No, but there is belief in an allegiance to the anachronistic view largely abandoned by other professions that all the responsibility for update rests with the individual.

7. Is the profession able to speak out with one voice on issues that affect it? No, many voices claim a right to be heard on just about every issue. With 377,046 participants, it may be that the Teachers Insurance Annuity Association (TIAA) is the most representative organization in the whole academic sector (TIAA-CREF, 1985).

8. Are there practice standards to define performance, ethics, and so on? No, there are almost no expressions of adequate performance, ethics, or obligations toward clients. There are, however, assertions of rights for practitioners (American Association of University Professors, 1973; Joughin, 1967).

By even the most generous interpretation and emendation of these very brief items, one must conclude that the academic profession at this time is poorly established and inattentive to the essential features of professionalization.

What is debilitating is not the paradox between the view that the profession resides only in the disciplines and the view that the profession comprehends the discipline, but rather that discussion of this important topic has stalled. And this discussion is important to the vitality of the profession as Houle (1981, p. 35) points out: "The first and most dominant characteristic (of a profession) is that as many members as possible . . . should be concerned with clarifying its defining function or functions. It is difficult but necessary to seek constantly to understand the structural tenets of a practitioner's work—those which give it focus and form." There is no shortage of literature on the structural tenets of academe: Shils's (1984) work on knowledge; the studies of Bess (1976), Blackburn and others (1978), Braxton and Toombs (1982) of role components; treatments of values by Merton (1973); and considerations of performance by Clark (1983) and Toombs and others (1985). There is a clear and workable definition of the profession in Parsons and Platt (1968, p. 109). "The academic profession is that group *primarily* concerned with the cognitive complex: with the advancement, perpetuation, and transmission of knowledge and with the development of cognitively significant competence." What is missing is attention to the interrelationships that form this mosaic into a coherent profession.

In sum, the profession *qua* profession is so weakly organized and so poorly represented in the framework of modern society that the vitality of able faculty members may never gain the recognition and influence it deserves.

Disciplines

The discipline, its activities, and its organizations have become the center of interest for many if not most faculty members. Ben-David (1984), especially in the pages of his revised work on scientists, gives a very complete history of this part of academic life. The parent organizations of long ancestry and the subspecialized organizations that have sprung up since World War II are one of the main professionalizing agencies of academic life, building specialized expertise into strong subcultures (Finkelstein, 1984). If the disciplinary associations were joined in some way to acknowledge the centrality of academic values and the worth of the academic enterprise, they might constitute a powerful expression of the profession. But they are not. As a result, the disciplines contribute unwittingly to the identity crisis of the academy and academics. Is it, for example, more prestigious to be called a chemist or to be called a chemistry professor? Is the image of "psychologist" more satisfying than the self-description, "professor of psychology"? Semantic differentials are among the minor signals of confusion in the identity of the academic profession. Faculty members identify with disciplines because they feel, and rightly so, the greater public acceptance of the specialist role and the mystique that goes with it.

Since there is no way for the disciplines to stand in joint representation of the profession as a whole, the key question becomes one of how well some degree of balance between the disciplines is maintained to serve the broad interest of learning, of *Wissenschaft* so to speak. And Flexner's (1930, p. 347) reminder is germane: "Yet *Wissenschaft* remains fundamental— fundamental to the solution of problems, fundamental to the operations of the industrialist. And more and more, as knowledge and life increases in complexity, an adequate provision for thought has also to be made." Within the university a balance between the different areas of knowledge and learning would seem a necessary consequence of the proposition that all knowledge is tentative. Part of the difficulty in perceiving and accepting the commonalities in the academic expression of all the disciplines arises because the presence of value-laden topics and threats to the academy is unevenly distributed among the disciplines. In the social sciences the protection of academic freedom is a constant need, while in the natural sciences it arises only periodically. The capacity to see clearly the dimension of threats to free inquiry is probably diminished by specialization unless one pauses occasionally to consider the whole academic landscape. It may be no accident that those who took the lead in defining the values of academe, largely between 1900 and 1930, were persons trained in the generalist tradition of scholarship then "professionalized" to the specialty of a discipline. Many avenues of learning must be maintained in a climate of mutual regard if all learning is to be sustained as a republic of scholars.

It has become more and more difficult for the academy to maintain a balanced view of knowledge. During the period of rapid expansion under National Defense Education Act fellowships, National Aeronautics and Space Administration funding, and National Science Foundation/National Institutes of Health fellowships and traineeships, many major research universities made conscious policy decisions to find ways of shifting funds into the humanities and social sciences so they would not be overwhelmed by natural science and technology. Much of the flexibility in federal funding that made such internal adjustment possible is now gone. The emphasis of the nuclear-space-defense age on natural science has been joined by new popularity for computer science and business. Funding sources, whether industrial, defense, or business, have very specific interests and are not disposed to give the university latitude in the application of grants, contracts, and awards. When we add to this inflexibility the rise of interest in career studies among undergraduates, significant kinds of disequilibrium begin to appear—not only horizontally across colleges and disciplines but vertically between undergraduate and graduate, between scholarship and research.

Let us project some of the current trends into the future and sketch out how these disciplinary distinctions may affect the academy as the imbalance of various areas of knowledge increases. First, the heavy and exclusive emphasis of the public mind on technology and certain aspects of the sciences shuts out any consideration of the full nature of education. Instrumental solutions of very short duration, creating and finding jobs for example, are the only evident objective. Funds targeted for single purposes, solving a technical problem for defense or industry for example, leave little room for consideration of related inquiry that may not have an immediate payoff or for the costly training of high-level manpower. Even more significant is the fact that the purposes of funding are decided and defined more by bodies and agents external to academic research, less by the state of knowledge; more by conditions of the market, less by questions to be explored. Such specific operations require universities to shift support patterns, services, equipment, and facilities in directions that are often not those of learning or of education and certainly not those of broad scholarship.

Parallel to these kinds of discipline-based phenomena in the university setting are the shifts in undergraduate majors that affect all institutions. The massive and well-documented movement to business, engineering, computer science, and a few other technical specialties has consequences that are as certain as they are discernible. The aims and structure of the curriculum in most of these fields are determined by conditions of practice and the market, not by faculty or scholars concerned with the forefront of knowledge or the knotty issues of the future. Evidence is found in the large number of articles on "what employers want" that crowd the current literature. For the undergraduate, the experience toward the baccalaureate must be seen as a somewhat artificial prelude to a real existence in a real world that lies outside the university.

Courses in these high-application areas must be taught by faculty with some exposure to and involvement in that world of practice. This is no place for teaching assistants, and the faculty salary level must be more related to the external labor market than to the academic salary structure. In turn this salary differential, euphemistically referred to as "market adjustment," encourages tuition differentials that generate philosophical questions about open options for students and the true nature of learning. Such a shift in emphasis toward one side of the curriculum has severe consequences for graduate study. Most of the so-called career fields rarely lead to graduate-level study and almost never to doctoral work. Graduate schools, already beleaguered by costs, are in for some very trying times in the next ten years.

In the membership figures for selected professional associations are found some of the signals of academic disequilibrium. In Table 1 the rising popularity of professional bodies wherein academics and nonacademic practitioners in a particular discipline meet is exemplified in the significant rise in membership of the American Chemical Society, the American Psychological Association, and the American Physical Society. The decline of those societies with high proportions of academics is equally apparent, as exemplified in the figures for the American Historical Association, the American Society for Engineering Education, and the Modern Language Association.

Putting the consequences of this imbalance together, we have the situation in which institutions are driven toward two (or more) levels of tuition and two (or more) levels of faculty salary plans. The effect is the creation of two classes of citizens in the academic community, one oriented to external values, the other to the intrinsic values of knowledge and learning. A declining graduate school, with pronounced leanings toward practical masters-level work, and research that is largely defined by outside interests

Table I. Disciplinary Professional Bodies: Membership 1960–1985

	1960	1970	1980	1985
American Psychological Association	18,215	30,839	50,933	60,131
American Chemical Society	92,193	114,323	120,400	134,449
American Historical Association	N/A	20,188	13,807	11,797
American Sociological Association	6,875	14,156	12,868	11,000
Modern Language Association	10,500	31,356	28,266	26,302
American Society for Engineering Education	9,120	12,157	13,081	9,810
American Political Science Association	N/A	N/A	13,075	12,673
American Physical Society	18,470	28,207	30,973	36,545

Source: Telephone Survey of Association Offices, July 1985.

are also in evidence. There is little that is fanciful in this scenario, much that has negative consequences for faculty vitality in the respective disciplines and for the collective vitality of the academic enterprise as a whole.

Institutions

The posture of the institution has a part in determining the outcomes and consequences of faculty vitality as well as a part in cultivating that vitality. It appears that, statewide systems and boards notwithstanding, the institution is once more the unit of destiny. There are *Three Thousand Futures* (Carnegie Council, 1981). Behind academics today stand nearly two decades in which the pressures of enrollment and inflation drove institutional leaders in the direction of management and trouble-shooting to the exclusion of all else. Reflecting on his twenty years of educational leadership, a college classmate recently observed, "I spent the first decade talking with architects and the second talking with lawyers."

Faculty members have not assumed any large role of participation in matters of budget, selecting students for admission, physical expansion, or institutional development. Since their area of primary concern, the curriculum, has altered somewhat in content but little in its structure, faculty members in general tend to hold themselves at some distance from institutional policy issues. The growing emphasis on each institution making its own way in its own environment presents an opportunity and a challenge to faculty as well as to institutional leaders. Several conditions would seem to indicate that this is an optimum time for faculty to seek new ways of participating in the boundary-spanning functions of the institution. There is, for example, much less guidance for higher education or even the disciplines from some grand federal strategy. Out of habit, academics will continue to look for federal policy directions in funding patterns of defense, National

Science Foundations, or other agencies and in the reorganization of departments like education, the interior, or agriculture. But the locus of policy and action has clearly shifted to the state level and to special constituencies in the regional and local realm.

This shift points to a second condition that makes faculty participation more necessary. Public understanding of what higher education is engaged with is very incomplete. At one pole of misunderstanding is the notion that higher education is not much different than K–12 systems. At the other is the view that higher education exists only as a part of science, health, industry, or agriculture. Institutions have not been strikingly effective in communicating what goes on in education to legislators, public leaders, the press, or even to alumni. Faculty involvement may contribute a solution to this formidable problem of presentation and persuasion.

Institutions have a responsibility, too, to make policies that build a broad base for professional vitality and development. At first glance, the programs of faculty development—instructional, organizational, and personal—appear to hold part of the answer. Experience in the 1970s and early 1980s tells us otherwise. These programs reached a peak about the time of Centra's study (1976), which provides an excellent benchmark. For the most part these efforts were framed to reflect a view of professional behavior that was in atrophy. They treated faculty members as if they were independent practitioners. Individual career advancement, individual instructional competence, and individual acquisition of skills and technique—those were typical objectives, though not always articulated in that specific a manner. Programs had few lines of connection with institutional leadership or central administration.

There are slight indications of change in data from a forthcoming study. Uwalaka (1985) presented to a sample of four-year institutions, liberal arts and comprehensive colleges those factors from Centra's study that carried high loadings. Academic officers were asked to indicate the level of "support" for each activity. The results are displayed in Table 2, and even though the comparison with Centra is not exact, some very interesting indications emerge. There is a rise in attention to items that fit the mission and direction of the institution. For example, computer training and audio-visual techniques are likely to be of significance in the whole curriculum, not just in a single faculty member's classes. Advising skills enhance the ability of the institution to convey its educational message. Performance ratings by peers and students serve the interests of the institution as well as those of individual faculty members. That, of course, is the key—congruence and coherence between institutional mission and faculty behavior. The principle has a long history illustrated in the early studies of "impact" on students, visible in the "peculiarly potent" institutions of Jacob's (1957) study, reiterated in several of the Carnegie Commission reports, and lately

Table 2. Professional Development Practices: Comparison of
Ratings from the Studies of Centra (1976) and Uwalaka (1985)

Practices	Rated "Effective" or "Very Effective" (Centra, 1976) N=315	Rated "Supported" or "Very Well Supported" (Uwalaka, 1985) N=178
Grants to faculty members for developing new or different approaches to courses or teaching	68%	55.7%
Visitation to other institutions (or to other parts of this institution to review educational programs or innovative projects)	49%	39.9%
Faculty exchange programs with other institutions (here, or abroad)	46%	20.2%
Faculty taking courses offered by colleagues	46%	50.1%
Personal counseling provided to individual faculty members on career goals and other personal development areas	50%	28.1%
Workshops or presentations that explore various methods or techniques of instruction	53%	66.2%
Workshops, seminars, or programs to acquaint faculty with the institution's mission, history, curriculum, and types of students enrolled	53%	50.5%
Workshops or programs to help faculty improve their academic advising and counseling skills	46%	54.5%
Workshops or seminars to help faculty improve their research and scholarly skills	45%	38.2%
Workshops or presentations that explore general issues or trends in education	42%	42.7%
Systematic ratings of instruction made by students and used to help improve faculty	46%	93.3%
Formal assessments made by colleagues for teaching or course improvement (visitations or use of assessment form)	42%	58.4%

Practices	Rated "Effective" or "Very Effective" (Centra, 1976) N=315	Rated "Supported" or "Very Well Supported" (Uwalaka, 1985) N=178
Systematic teaching or course evaluations made by an administrator for improvement purposes	45%	54.5%
Faculty with expertise consulting with other faculty on teaching or course improvement	57%	46.7%
"Master teachers" or senior faculty working closely with new or "apprentice" teachers	56%	22.5%
Professional and personal development plans (sometimes called a growth contract) for individual faculty members	57%	31.4%
Specialists on campus to assist faculty in use of audio-visual aids in instruction, including closed-circuit television	57%	65.8%
Assistance to faculty in the use of instructional technology as a teaching aid (programmed learning or computer-assisted instruction)	50%	69.1%
Specialists to assist faculty in constructing tests or evaluating student performances	49%	21.9%
Specialists to assist individual faculty members in instructional or course development by consulting on course objectives and course design	53%	22.5%
Specialists to help the faculty develop teaching skills such as lecturing or leading discussions, or to encourage use of different teaching-learning strategies, such as individualized instruction	50%	21.9%

Note: Centra reported the percentages of institutions that estimated each item as either "effective" or "very effective." The 1985 study reports percentages of institutions estimating each item as "supported" or "very well supported."

confirmed by Astin's (1985) research findings. To the extent that institutions can support a professional development program that acknowledges the breadth of faculty interest within the scope of institutional mission, they will spread the consequences of vitality more effectively.

Conclusion

To assess the larger setting in which faculty vitality is interpreted, three boundary-spanning functions have been reviewed. These are organizations in which faculty members themselves play a significant role. The *profession* is poorly established in comparison with other professions and has been indifferent to its own professionalization. The *disciplines,* which played so large a part in gaining strength for the modern view of specialized expertise and for the structure of departments, are unable to come together to support the academic value structure in an effective manner. Across the disciplines serious imbalances are evident that may damage academic claims to the full province of knowledge. *Institutions* now on their own in localized environments will be required to construct a more comprehensive program of explanation and presentation. Faculty members have a major part to play, but there is little provision for their role in the policy structure of most institutions and small disposition on the part of a faculty trained to an individualistic view. Institutions are just beginning to integrate the full range of professional development into the mainstream of policy.

One should not read this critical analysis of the profession, the disciplines, and institutional practices as an accusation of ineffectiveness. Institutions and their faculties have been very effective in advancing many of the significant areas of modern life, from changes in social values to economic development and scientific excellence. But it has come at a cost to that comprehensive professionalism that will be an absolute necessity if academic life, the major locus of intellectual activity, is to regain the support it requires and the acknowledgement it deserves. A summary of how it has been possible to be effective without that coherence is nicely provided by Touraine (1974, p. 161), a French scholar writing for the Carnegie Commission. "To sum up, the dominant feature of the academic system is not a professionalism defined by values and autonomous organization but rather the complementariness between strengthening the university's own power and a scientific development linking more and more closely the big universities to social power. Professionalism, rather than being a fundamental principle, is the unifying factor between these two tendencies. . . ." The line of argument here is, of course, that such an instrumental and scattered view of professional identity is no longer adequate.

Is there no prospect of moving away from these relentless forces of separatism? Fortunately there are signs that the collective aspects of academic action may have passed through the nadir. First, there are significant movements toward combinations of disciplines into something like functional "areas" of study and application. These are quite different from the "area studies" movement of the 1950s and 1960s in the social sciences and are more deeply rooted than most efforts at interdisciplinarity. They arise from fundamental changes in the structure of scientific knowledge. Material science, biotechnology along with the sounder expressions of environmental science and policy studies, can lead eventually to a broader base of understanding and regard than the disciplines have been able to foster. Second, with the changes in the times has come a new generation of academic leadership that is oriented to the educational effects of performance and programs. Third, there are now in view serious shortages of academic talents in fields that seemed unlikely prospects for shortage a decade ago (foreign languages and mathematics for example). The cuts in graduate support and the message of poor prospects may have worked too well. A more stable view and a longer planning horizon for the development of professional competence may be the result.

What still remains is the too casual interest and indifferent participation of faculty in the agencies of collective identity. No one else is able to present adequately the range and meaning of the enterprise of learning. However good the work of individuals may be, there is no other guarantee of public understanding or acceptance, especially in a media-soaked society with a short attention span.

References

American Association of University Professors. *Policy Documents and Reports.* Washington, D.C.: AAUP, 1973.

Anderson, G. L. "Trends in Education for the Profession." *Higher Education Report 7.* Washington, D.C.: ERIC, 1974.

Astin, A. W. *Achieving Educational Excellence.* San Francisco: Jossey-Bass. 1985.

Ben-David, J. *The Scientist's Role in Society.* (Rev. ed.) Chicago: University of Chicago Press, 1984.

Bess, J. L. "Organization Implications of Faculty Role/Activity Preferences." ED 134089. Paper presented at American Educational Research Association, April 1976.

Blackburn, R. T., Behymer, C. E. and Hall, D. E. "Correlates of Faculty Publication." *Sociology of Education, 51* (April 1978), 132–141.

Bowen, H. R., and Schuster, J. H. *American Professors: A National Resource Imperiled.* New York: Oxford University Press, 1986.

Braxton, J. M., and Toombs, W. "Faculty Uses of Doctoral Training." *Research in Higher Education,* 1982, *16* (3), 265–281.

Bucher, R., and Strauss, A. "Professions in Process." *American Journal of Sociology,* 1961, *66,* 325–334.

Carnegie Council. *Three Thousand Futures.* San Francisco: Jossey-Bass, 1981.

82

Centra, J. "Faculty Development Practices in U.S. Colleges and Universities." Project Report 76–30. Princeton, N.J.: Educational Testing Service, 1976.

Clark, B. R. *The Higher Education System*. Berkeley: University of California Press, 1983.

Finkelstein, M. J. *The American Academic Profession: A Synthesis of Social Scientific Inquiry Since World War II*. Columbus: Ohio State University Press, 1984.

Flexner, A. *Universities: American, English, German*. New York: Oxford University Press, 1968. (Originally published in 1930.)

Goode, W. J. "The Theoretical Limits of Professionalization." In A. Etzioni (Ed.), *The Semi-Professions and Their Organization*. New York: Free Press, 1969.

Hickson, D. J., and Thomas, M. W. "Professionalization in Britain: A Preliminary Measurement." *Sociology*, 1969, *3*, 37–53.

Houle, C. O. *Continuing Learning in the Professions*. San Francisco: Jossey-Bass, 1981.

Hughes, E. C. *Education for the Professions of Medicine, Law, Theology, and Social Welfare*. New York: McGraw-Hill, 1973.

Hutchins, R. M. *The Higher Learning in America*. New Haven, Conn.: Yale University Press, 1936.

Jacob, P. E. *Changing Values in College*. New York: Harper & Row, 1957.

Joughin, L. *Academic Freedom and Tenure*. Madison: University of Wisconsin Press, 1967.

Ladd, E. C., Jr., and Lipset, S. M. *The Divided Academy*. Carnegie Commission. New York: McGraw-Hill, 1975.

Liacouras, P. "AAUP Censures 4 Institutions: 50 Now on List," *Chronicle of Higher Education*, June 26, 1985.

Merton, R. K. *The Sociology of Science*. Chicago: University of Chicago Press, 1973.

Parsons, T., and Platt, G. M. *The American Academic Profession: A Pilot Study*. Cambridge, Mass.: Harvard University Press, 1968.

Schein, E. H. *Professional Education*. New York: McGraw-Hill, 1972.

Shils, *The Academic Ethic*. Chicago: University of Chicago Press, 1984.

Smutz, W. D., and others. "The Practice Audit Model." Monograph, The Pennsylvania State University, 1981.

Teachers Insurance Annuity Association–College Retirement Equities Fund. *Research Dialogues*. Issue no. 4. New York: Educational Research Unit, June 1985.

Toombs, W., and others. "Modifying Faculty Roles to Institutionalize Continuing Professional Education." *Research in Higher Education*, 1985, *22* (1), 93–109.

Touraine, A. *The Academic System in American Society*. Carnegie Commission. New York: McGraw-Hill, 1974.

Uwalaka, O. A. "Professional Development and Institutional Support: A Study of the Pattern of Variation and Determinants of Institutional Support for Professional Development of Faculty." Forthcoming doctoral dissertation, Pennsylvania State University.

Veblen, T. *The Higher Learning in America*. New York: Huebsh, 1918.

Vollmer, H. M., and Mills, D. L. *Professionalization*. Englewood Cliffs, N.J.: Prentice-Hall, 1966.

Znaniecki, F. *Social Role of the Man of Knowledge*. New York: Columbia University Press, 1940.

William Toombs is director of the Center for the Study of Higher Education, Pennsylvania State University, in University Park. His research has focused on faculty, curriculum, and continuing education in the professions.

A broad definition of the kinds of excellence to be supported created a "critical mass" of faculty committed to continuing professional development.

Faculty Incentives at the College of Charleston: A Case Study

Paul J. Hamill, Jr.

This is a case study of the use of small grants as faculty incentives at the College of Charleston, which has maintained a highly successful program of faculty development since 1976. The small grants, some given after peer review and some given as discretionary funds, proved to be a flexible instrument for meeting various needs. They were part of a package of methods and incentives used to further faculty development in areas ranging from research to management skills. This case history, then, views the small grant as a catalytic incentive, a method for vitalizing the larger, continuing incentives for faculty growth: love of learning, love of teaching, love of fellowship, concern for students, personal autonomy, prestige, power, and economic rewards.

I describe the College of Charleston program as an effort to meet a series of challenges, each of which developed from success at an earlier stage. This allows discussion of the many ways in which small grants can be—and were—used as incentives for meeting different institutional and personal needs. Each stage in the program, then, is described as facing a distinct problem with new or refined mechanisms. The tradeoffs or characteristic

R. G. Baldwin (Ed.). *Incentives for Faculty Vitality.* New Directions for Higher Education. no. 51. San Francisco: Jossey-Bass, September 1985.

tensions involved in the solution are discussed; outcomes are sketched; and finally, I comment on general questions raised by each stage of the program.

Phase 1: Establishing Faculty Development

The College of Charleston, which traces its origin to 1770, was a small private liberal arts college of about 450 students when it became affiliated with the state of South Carolina in 1969. The college reached a stable enrollment of over 5300 students (about 4200 undergraduate full-time equivalents) in 1975–76 and acquired a regular faculty of over 200 professors, mostly doctorate holders in their first teaching post.

When John M. Bevan became academic vice-president in 1975, he saw that the college was at a historic point in its development because the young faculty members were setting patterns of professional activity and expectations of quality that would likely characterize the institution until the end of the century. He appointed George Morgan, who had been an innovative dean at Hiram College, to direct faculty development and set up a grants office. I replaced Morgan in 1979, but continued to build on his excellent foundation. Both of us were rightly perceived as speaking for the vice-president concerning one of his highest priorities.

Bevan set up a fund of $10,000 for mini-grants and another $7500 in discretionary budgets. He also set up an advisory committee of faculty members to work with Morgan in support of professional development, teaching improvement, and research. The maximum individual grant was set at $1500, but most awards went no higher than $1,000. Funds were increased to about $30,000 in 1977–78, including $10,000 from the College of Charleston Foundation, used mainly for faculty traveling to give papers and for retreats and special projects. A process of grant proposal, committee review, recommendation to Bevan, and award by the president was created.

Morgan urged the committee to stretch available funds by recommending as many worthwhile projects as possible at absolute minimum funding levels. This caused some disagreement, but it was wise; grants were more widely spread among faculty, and the incentive to find external funds, with Morgan's help, was maximized. A few years later, when I asked reviewers to rank proposals by quality on a first read through and then discuss budget separately, the result was similar—the committee pared the best proposals as far as possible, to provide at least some funds for every worthwhile request. It is worth adding that while faculty members possess a deep-seated belief in competition and a sensible distaste for working on too-slender budgets, the purpose of faculty development funding, even in research, is not so much to increase the world's store of learning as to keep the faculty alive. Competition and review are necessary to ensure seriousness and rigor, but once these are achieved, the weaker project may do as much for the college and its proposer as the stronger one. Obviously, there is a fine line to be drawn, requiring tactful advocacy by administrators and experience on the part of faculty.

At this stage of the faculty development program, the characteristic tensions were, for faculty, the difficulty of judging different kinds of projects, learning to review proposals without acting as advocates of one's own department or faction, dealing with the insufficient size of the grants (the loudest complainers were not the best-ranked proposers), and responding to the complaint from outside the committees about the perceived new pressure for research and innovation.

The faculty moved almost immediately to make the faculty research and development committee a standing faculty body, as an assertion of independence. However, Bevan and Morgan set the budget, Morgan guided procedures and worked with proposers to develop proposals, and Bevan reviewed grant recommendations before the president received them, so that the process remained closely integrated with the vice-president's goals for the faculty.

By way of outcomes, younger faculty members in particular became interested in working with Morgan on external grant applications. In-house workshops such as one on Piaget led to discussion groups and eventually to external proposals for improving curriculum. As a further outcome, the research interests of many faculty members, especially younger professors, were buttressed by the existence of a committee and awards to encourage them. Professional activity was, arguably, bound to increase if even modest incentives were offered and disincentives lessened; however, activity increased with dramatic speed, reflecting a coherent vision of the characteristics of a strong undergraduate faculty.

Special faculty incentives must be consistent with the larger message concerning institutional values, rewards, and expectations sent by key leaders, such as the president or academic vice-president. These officers guarantee that success will be weighed in tenure and promotion, and that innovative risk takers will be protected in turf conflicts. I would add with respect to mechanisms that over the long term, successful faculty development requires both peer review processes and a discretionary budget. The first is needed for credibility and assurance of quality, and also in order to involve faculty members who may be suspicious of the administration. The second is needed for decisions that must be made quickly, for high-risk decisions about persons or programs, or to fit precisely with a plan for external grant development. In our experience, moreover, senior faculty members often wish to negotiate with the president or vice-president before applying through peer procedures for personal upgrading of skills in order to ensure that the application will not be seen as an admission of weakness. One mechanism may be formal and the other informal, but if the need for both can be recognized and the outcomes evaluated together, as at the College of

Charleston, the faculty will be more willing to support new initiatives to match the goals.

Phase 2: Developing Balanced Strength with Lilly Funds

Having gathered a second advisory committee, Bevan successfully approached the Lilly Endowment with a proposal for a broad faculty development program that the college would continue after Lilly funds ended. As it turned out, the Lilly grant did more than pay for a splendid program; it also strengthened the college's increasing commitment through several years of periodic budget crises, so that faculty development had a chance to establish its worth as an ongoing priority.

Bevan's philosophy of broad development was expressed in the categories of activities funded under the grant, which were categories of excellence in the faculty member rather than specific activities. The categories included: professional development, which included college-funded research, and Lilly-funded retraining or special training in one's discipline; teaching improvement, in the form of seminars and use of consultants; interdisciplinary learning, such as cooperative course development, entering new fields to enrich one's own discipline, and interdisciplinary seminars on current problems; contact with nonacademic professionals, which came to include school-college cooperation; administrative development, which included training departmental chairs, offering retreats, and covering costs of the external evaluator, William O'Connell.

Two committees helped to administer the funds: an advisory "Lilly Committee" for all of the above categories except research; and the standing faculty committee, which became the Research Committee. Certain special projects, "matches" for external grants, most retreats and administrative development activities, and travel to workshops like the National Science Foundation Chautauquas were authorized directly by the vice-president or assistant vice-president. Major proposals (over $500) for workshops on campus, new course development, study at other universities, and so on, came before one of the committees.

Tensions is too negative a word for the dynamic that this program set up. There was always ambiguity in the roles of the two committees, partly because the vision of flexible excellence that underlay the structure did not fit anyone's stereotypes. So many kinds of activity were visible as expressions of professional growth that constant communication, matching of interests, encouragement of the timid, and restraining of enthusiasts kept Morgan and myself busy. However, results were widely scrutinized, and new sources of aid, including external grants, developed as predicted, so that the tensions were creative rather than destructive. The "Research" Committee represented a dramatic change in that faculty members who had not felt encouraged to publish now possessed a forum for espousing research, which received ever increasing support. The assistant vice-president did not vote on the Research Committee, but controlled its budget; precisely because I did not vote, I could act aggressively as program officer and advocate, proposing new priorities, negotiating on behalf of the committee with applicants, and feeding back criticisms of proposals. By requiring this accountability, I could also counteract the occasional displays of disciplinary bias in committee votes.

The multitude of categories and mixture of peer review and discretionary modes of action allowed us to avoid being paralyzed by debate over different kinds of excellence, as noted earlier. True, we debated regularly on whether to fund excellent researchers fully or to fund meagerly so that we could aid weaker colleagues in upgrading skills. We puzzled over how much the improvement of advising skills deserved funding as compared with course development, and we puzzled over other questions of the same sort. As I wrote later (Hamill, 1982), faculty members are ideally suited to judge ambiguous categories, and despite some complaints of mixing apples with oranges, they made sensible recommendations each year.

The context of development sharpened the review of proposals. Research proposals by established scholars were down-rated if they did not include movement toward external funding or conquest of some new area of knowledge. We wanted our grants to be the backup option for such professors, and by 1983 had formalized the requirement that possible external funding be discussed in the proposal. The same proposal by a new faculty member or one who had been inactive might receive higher ratings. Similarly, we did not fund new course development unless a new technology, interdepartmental cooperation, or other special feature was involved because new courses are created continually as a matter of course. "Hard" costs, for example, travel or supplies, were funded before living stipends.

We evaluated individual mini-grants through a required final report, and long-term impact by assigning a faculty subcommittee to review outcomes several years later. The results were remarkable. Publications rose from about twelve articles in 1975 to a stable level of about three hundred presentations, publications, and exhibits per year. By 1983, many books and national presentations were included in this figure. In addition, three hundred or so community presentations of a professional nature were being recorded yearly, such as volunteer counseling and teacher workshops.

A further outcome was that, during this period, numerous faculty members sought to articulate and improve the college's commitment to research, advising, distinguished teaching, or curriculum improvement, as they saw the need. Dr. Bevan's style was to encourage dialogue and, when possible, to encourage positive confrontation: Persons who objected to a program or who saw an unmet need were generally invited to propose alternatives. For example, in several instances, persons who complained about perceived misdirection of Lilly awards were invited to join the committee, and they did so. In retrospect, it is clear that both a positive ferment and negative feelings arose because some senior faculty members, who were slow to use the new incentives but gradually did so, were losing status as younger faculty members progressed, aided by mini-grants. This would have occurred in any event, but the available incentives made the process more constructive. So broad was the definition of possible excellences that a large "critical mass" of faculty members oriented to continuing professional development was created, which later carried considerable weight in faculty governance.

I have hinted that interdisciplinary development turned out to be a particularly valuable category. We found that many of the best research scholars were, and are, interdisciplinary; as fields change, the best scholars need to pass the boundaries of their formal training, so that they are the least threatened by change and the most interested in new connections. The Lilly or nonresearch committee included many of the top researchers. They understood early that their special interests could receive support only if all faculty members could see ways to develop. Moreover, they were not tempted to think that all of their colleagues would fit into a single mold of excellence. This point came home to me when a distinguished senior faculty member, notable for research, complained in her first year on one committee that too much money was going for such "soft" projects as improving one's disciplinary knowledge and internships with off-campus professionals. The majority overrode her objection after listening respectfully. The next year, a fervent young scholar recently out of graduate school made the same objection. "You don't see," said the senior faculty member, "When I came here there was no money for research. Now we have it and we will have more, because all the people who won't do research have other projects, and they will stand for research funds because they have a share."

Finally—and this point is easily neglected—teaching innovation in each discipline has a cutting edge just as research does. The committees required that new curricular methods reflect current developments. As a result, a significant number of publications and external grants that sprang from the mini-grant program dealt with course improvement or evaluation.

Phase 3: Teaching the Management of Incentives

The success of faculty development raised new questions: First, how were individuals and the college to continue faculty development without the ever-increasing infusion of special funds? The college had committed itself to keeping the funding at the level of combined Lilly and state funds when the grant ended, but those sums would clearly fail to satisfy the need engendered by success. More profoundly, how could incentives be managed collegewide so that, day in and day out, faculty development would remain a priority, a continuing source of creativity and flexibility, when administrators and agendas changed?

At the annual chairpersons' retreat, consultants John Centra and Grace French-Lazovik explored the role of the chair in faculty evaluation and development, stressing this role as the single most crucial index of effectiveness. Bevan explored strategies in course assignment, release time, yearly counseling of each professor, varied committee and special assignments, and other methods by which the chair could guide development and explore new initiatives (Bevan, 1982).

Following the retreat, French-Lazovik and a faculty group reviewed evaluation procedures, especially student surveys. To address the continually growing need for funds and link it with an incentive, agreement was reached that a portion of indirect costs from grants would return to academic affairs for faculty development, with the proposing department first in line for the funds. To encourage departmental management, "banking" of credit for service and independent study direction was introduced so that department chairs could offer release time for research and special projects. A group of six individual directed studies was declared to be equivalent to a standard course. Pooling each department's independent studies in sections of six students allowed documentation of the "bank" on which the faculty members could draw as they requested time for specific projects.

Chairs were encouraged to prioritize use of travel funds and to seek ways to use student aid assignments to aid faculty development (for example, as research assistants). Finally, a new mechanism for academic-year small grants, "Lilly Fellowships," was designed to encourage departmental release times, research by new faculty, and external grant-seeking.

A faculty member would apply for replacement costs of one course release time plus project funds, usually totaling about $2500. This "fellowship" was treated as honorific; it required the department's support by nomination and "match" by a second release time that was not replaced but achieved by managing course assignments inventively. In research, first priority went to those whose extra work would allow production of an external grant proposal to a specified agency. The next priority was new faculty who could "hit the ground running" in research and grant planning. Similar conditions of award applied for innovative service projects: on-campus impact and, ideally, prospects of external funding for continuation were required. We concluded, incidentally, that one release time in a four-course, twelve-credit-per-semester teaching load is not useful except to relieve stress, for Parkinson's Law assures us that the time will be filled up with reading the memos and straightening the files one has previously ignored. Releasing two courses does make a difference, especially if the remaining courses represent only one preparation, and the professor deliberately breaks routine by declining committee assignments and, if possible, switching offices. The nomination and match provisions were intended to ensure a positive departmental attitude—colleague resentment can be a powerful disincentive—and to provide the department chair and applicant leverage to consider unusual course assignment patterns. To give two examples: A chemistry professor, awarded a Lilly Fellowship, was assigned an advanced course and a laboratory in his research area as his two courses. Teaching both on Monday, he was able to spend the rest of the week in research, achieving an "in-house sabbatical." A mathematics professor, who normally taught three four-credit courses, took on a single enlarged section of a four-credit course, with excellent student graders, as her entire load.

All but two of the first ten "Lilly Fellows" eventually obtained external support for later stages of their projects. By 1982–83, most departments systematically awarded release time, and research and development committee "Grants in Time" were made a regular category of support. Return of indirect costs to faculty development proved a useful incentive, not because the amounts were large, but because the applicant and chair were often able to note that Professor X's travel to a particular convention was made possible by Professor Y's grant—so that the status of the innovator within the department and the chair, who supported grants, was improved. A variant of this incentive was introduced later, under acting Vice-President Hugh Haynsworth, who had been a leader in faculty development as a department chair. A matching fund for external equipment grants was set up. If the grants were not funded, or if they were still pending when college funds had to be used or returned to the state coffers, the matching funds would be turned over to the applicant's department for equipment purchase.

Phase 4: New Options and Incentives

The efforts recorded so far had created an atmosphere in which almost no serious idea for professional growth was flatly turned down. When internal grant funds were not available or appropriate, negotiation of new assignments or pursuit of external sources was encouraged, with much matching and mixing of sources. To give a modest example: A faculty member who proposed late in the budget year to bring a student team to the Model Organization of African States received a small grant from Faculty Development on the condition that he persuade other offices—student government, students affairs, and so on—to match it, which he did. The college made a successful showing, winning several awards, and student government picked up the activity as a regular budget item. To offer an example with community repercussions: A faculty member who created a nationally significant series on avant-garde music at the Spoleto Festival explained how the Lilly funds helped him to engage in the same enterpreneurial program-building: "The total worth of the project, that is, how much a similar independent project would cost without college assistance, could be conservatively estimated at between twenty-five and thirty thousand dollars. The amount of actual funding received was only about ten thousand dollars. Except for the two thousand dollars of Lilly fund money, the funds have been tightly controlled by the funders. The Lilly money . . . was what allowed me to have the desperately needed flexibility to present a rounded, fully comprehensive series."

Success created a new set of challenges on which Bevan (1979) reflected, and which were debated by the Lilly and the Research committees. Once the incentives for growth in standard faculty roles are introduced, and once many have tenure, how can growth be sustained over a period of years? Mechanisms such as in-house fellowships or in-house sabbaticals, occurring between formal sabbatical years, offer an obvious partial solution.

As a starting point, Bevan suggested that the opportunity to take on leadership in areas of special strength is itself an incentive. Individuals discover that they have special skills that deserve recognition and through which they may provide leadership to peers in such areas as advising techniques, teaching methods, and community service. But how could faculty members be given the chance to exercise this leadership? There are not enough formal administrative roles to provide channels; this is especially true in an institution in creative ferment. Whatever new options were considered had to be useful against burnout or isolation of specialized faculty members; they had to help individuals to prepare to change jobs, including leaving academe. New, individually tailored professional options were clearly needed.

A parallel dialogue was occurring under the leadership of Frank van Aalst, dean of career development, in the Student Affairs Committee of the Charleston Higher Education Consortium. The student affairs staff persons in the Charleston area successfully proposed a two-year development program to the Fund for the Improvement of Postsecondary Education, mixing elements of familiar professional development, techniques of career development counseling, and themes from literature on adult development (Kay and van Aalst, 1984).

The college undertook several career planning retreats for faculty, led by myself, van Aalst, and George Haborak, vice-president of student affairs, and Suzanne Moore, a professor of Spanish. The faculty career planning retreats are discussed elsewhere (see Lovett and others, 1984). We learned that most attendees really needed a chance to explore their options frankly. Discussing their earlier careers and the option of leaving academe led most professors to a strong recommitment to academe. We learned that, at "midlife," concrete family concerns must often be discussed explicitly—families with dual careers are not very mobile, for example. We learned that faculty members have typically had little chance to discuss the organizational milieu of higher education, that most have no comparative perspective, and that a crust of graduate school myths and coffee lounge truisms had to be addressed and broken through before serious thinking about careers could take place. When these steps were accomplished, the question of what options or opportunities one institution actually offers loomed large. It became clear that the retreat leaders saw many unmet institutional needs, and a broad scope for lateral or peer leadership, whereas faculty rarely thought in these terms. Therefore, a series of small grants was awarded, with Haynesworth's approval, for "internships": administrative assignments structured as learning experiences, in which the faculty applicant posed a problem that related to professional development but was also a college need. An administrator agreed to supervise and also to include the intern in staff activities and to provide half the costs; the applicant's department chair agreed to the arrangement; and formal evaluation by the applicant and the supervisor were required. Among other benefits, scheduling an end to the project allowed for failure without severe penalty.

As it happened, the first four interns were all placed with Sue Sommer, dean of continuing education. Working with her, a business professor developed professional development programs with local banks; a Spanish professor developed business people's institutes in international trade and English as a second language; a mathematics professor set up computer courses for middle-schoolers on a self-supporting basis; and a professor of education established cooperative staff development planning among regional school districts, following which she set up courses to fulfill the joint plans. Because markets were identified, permanent staff positions were created to continue two of these projects.

Personal career planning and formal and informal contracts for development, as well as strong emphasis on teaching the faculty to develop their own sources, marked this phase of the College of Charleston program. In special cases, small grants were used for required subventions for scholarly presses or to aid training that would enable a professor to develop consulting skills.

In seeking external grants, which were clearly necessary to extend faculty growth and provide funds for innovation, special emphasis was placed on finding those grants that could involve the faculty broadly, as the Lilly award had. A pilot grant from the National Endowment for the Humanities, followed by a grant for fostering coherence in the curriculum; a grant from the Office of Education for internationalizing the curriculum; National Science Foundation funding for local course development and later for materials development for teachers; and Exxon funding for computer faculty training all fit this description. Using existing faculty development mechanisms for proposing and reporting when possible, these programs have shown remarkable success. It should be said, in addition, that grant-seeking was encouraged because setting up and running grants is one way of developing leadership and budgeting skills and developing a portfolio for internal or external mobility.

At one review of summer grant applications, the Research Committee noted that a rather small pool of relatively weak applicants was to be considered. As we examined the roster of faculty members, we recognized that this was not a mark of failure. Broad-based grants such as that from the National Endowment for the Humanities, summer research work at local science facilities, several international travel courses, teaching for the innovative Governor's School, and individual fellowships and grants had provided funds for many faculty members, and a core of the remainder were needed for the college's large summer school. In short, the internal pool was weak because many faculty members had discovered various other options.

An ideal mix of applicants, I concluded, consists of strong scholars who have tried to obtain external funds but, for the moment, have not succeeded; applicants planning external proposals (their projects seem incomplete and must be defended during review); new faculty members seeking to build a record of funding, who should be pressed to write exemplary proposals for the practice; a few applications representing new or unorthodox directions for established professors (at least one reviewer will want to rule these ineligible); and applications by the weakest faculty members who are just beginning to exhibit vitality. As I said earlier of competition, the purpose of small grants, as of similar incentives, is to make the institution grow toward definite goals. If the goal is a general strengthening of faculty, the broadest possible spread of benefits brings up the general level. If research capacity or reputation is the goal, different criteria apply. If grant development is the aim, the focus must be on project development, and review simply ensures that the work thus far is rigorous. There should be a provision for meeting the special needs of the current period: competitions on computer use, for instance, or international learning. When incentives are managed in this way, the strength and promise of different projects is seen freshly, and the balance of publishable scholarship with personal learning, curricular development, and special kinds of service is more easily struck.

Phase 5: Incentives in the Context of Planning

In 1982 the administrative structure of the College of Charleston was changed to allow the president greater opportunity for external speaking and fund-seeking. Dr. Bevan had left the academic vice-presidency in 1981 to head the Charleston Higher Education Consortium. The newly defined position of provost, including the duties of the vice-president, was assumed by Jacquelyn A. Mattfeld. She reaffirmed the importance of faculty development and faculty incentives, and in addition began working successfully to raise pay scales across the board. One of her key tasks was to lead in developing institution-wide, participative planning and management procedures. In the context of planning, faculty development took on a slightly new look.

The new associate provost, Gerald Gibson, who had been a leader among department chairs in faculty development, took over faculty development, and led the Research and Development Committee to define more rigorously the categories of funding—research, professional improvement, curricular development, and so on. He and the committee clarified guidelines for writing proposals and increased the maximum grant amounts because the small size of awards had now become a disincentive. "Grants in Time," providing replacement costs for release time, summer stipends in lieu of summer teaching salary, grants in aid for direct project costs, and "starter grants" for new faculty were defined and awarded in three annual competitions. "Starter grants," which could be requested by a new professor just after being hired were seen by department chairs as useful in competing with research institutions.

The new context of planning generally shifts innovation to that process. Departments analyze and project their professional and curricular needs more broadly than would have been possible in earlier years, and they frequently specify that internal or external grants will be sought to meet their goals. While faculty internships in administration have not been continued, the provost has created a number of special assignments, such as organizing faculty computer training, which include travel to other sites, off-campus workshops, and other training features. In addition, staff lines have been increased, especially in student development areas. Faculty members who have moved into these positions were active in the "new options" retreats and other activities. The college is embarking on an untraditional self-study, focused on planning, which will provide many faculty members with leadership experiences and an impetus for new initiatives. The keynotes of planning are likely to be student body development and financial development, for which an excellent faculty is needed and available.

Grant-seeking in this period has continued to increase, and private fund-seeking is on the upswing with considerable faculty involvement. If there are new tensions in the area of faculty incentives, they are, first, that due to success, a high level of support is continually needed, outstripping the increased budgets, so that worthy projects are declined; second, that the flexibility of faculty development incentives for innovation has decreased, at least within the peer-reviewed part of the program; and finally, that there is less direct connection between applying internally and applying externally for funds. Nevertheless, the role of department chairs as managers whose key duties include faculty formation and external fund-seeking has been reaffirmed and extended. Faculty evaluation standards now include stiffer requirements for professional development; teaching effectiveness is defined to include effectiveness in advising and collateral kinds of teaching; and department chairs are evaluated, in part, on their ability to seek or encourage others to seek external funds.

Conclusion

By way of conclusion, let me reflect briefly on incentives and then summarize the ideas that proved successful at the College of Charleston. I stated earlier that small grants, like most of the incentives that one can manage readily, are catalytic: They are small or momentary changes in the condition of one professor's career or one college's atmosphere that set off reactions in favor of larger incentives. Commonly these catalytic incentives revive all the greater incentives to some degree, so that those moved by economic dissatisfaction become restless and, we hope entrepreneurial; those moved by love of learning or prestige begin new inquiry; those who love teaching or interaction with students feel enfranchised to renew their commitment; those who love power see new avenues for gaining authority. The actual incentives triggered depend equally on the individual and on the guiding vision of the president, provost, or dean who stands behind the program, insisting on a particular match-up between individual motives and the college's goals.

When I directed faculty career retreats, two facts were striking: first, that it was a liberating experience for the faculty to review the incentives or motives for which they started their careers, for which they now worked, and for which they might work in other fields. What might be called the grand incentives—money, for example—are involved in the large career choices, especially the choice to leave academe. Within academe, economic benefits are matters of rather small pay differentials in most institutions. For some faculty, who are the single source of support for their family, the financial incentive is crucial, but the problem is also a family problem; for others, the incentive is almost wholly symbolic in the short term. It follows that most of the incentives that can be managed internally, and most incentives that the faculty can and will discuss, offer ways for faculty members to recommit themselves to academic life, by means of new tasks or new status. That recommitment, which is an assertion of control over one's life and of responsibility for one's close fellows, is in itself an important reward.

The underlying discovery was that, in general, the motives for which most faculty members entered college teaching are still powerful, but require new outlets. Love of learning and pride in it, love of teaching, a taste for combined shelter and autonomy, and a powerful sociability are enduring traits. Molding incentives to enhance these traits, which college or university faculty careers should unabashedly reflect, is not only an ideal way to manage, but the only rational way over the long term.

The guiding ideas that explain this case history, I believe, are these:

1. Incentives such as small grants are catalytic, allowing the faculty to act on the greater, less flexible incentives that men and women live for.

2. Catalytic incentives work best when faculty members are able to act on them with as much freedom and consciousness of the meaning of their choices as possible. For that reason, the most systematic rigorous program will also seem highly personalized and may seem to encourage self-indulgence.

3. Because resources always fall short and because freedom is an incentive in itself, incentives such as small grants and staff help should be designed to enable faculty members to find their own resources.

4. Leadership in this context requires confrontation, negotiation, constant reaffirmation of ground rules, and some discretionary control of resources.

5. Both peer review and discretionary action are needed.

6. Both peer review and discretionary action need constant review in light of long- and short-term goals. The faculty must take part in this evaluation of goals, or they will be guided by tribal myths, not college needs, in judging good or poor professional development.

7. There should be an arsenal of means or incentives and likewise a variety of goals and styles of excellence. This allows many constituencies to support change and leaves room for failures in the context of overall success.

8. A research spirit, that is insistent on staying current and on fresh learning, is especially important in curricular and teaching improvement.

9. Incentives do not work without management. Small grants, for example, support specific goals if a program officer suggests projects, helps the faculty mold them, advocates, negotiates, provides feedback, and insists on evaluating progress.

10. Special incentives need to be integrated with central, ongoing functions. At the College of Charleston, for instance, faculty development is directly linked to evaluation for tenure and promotion; to evaluation of the department chair's effectiveness; to grant-seeking and advancement; and to planning.

11. Publicity is important, both external, in the form of recognition by newspaper or alumni publications and internal, in the form of newsletters, corridor interviews, and praise at faculty meetings. Faculty should be urged to tell their own stories of success through professional presentations or publications.

12. Never close all options. If a professor has an unworkable idea or a poorly conceived proposal, tell him or her so plainly. But if there is a spark of promise, or even a serious interest in taking some action, suggest alternate sources, alternate avenues, or useful people to talk to. Many a poor idea has been followed by a good one, because the proposer kept exploring.

References

Bevan, J. M. "Faculty Evaluation and Institutional Rewards." In W. O'Connell, Jr. (Ed.), *Improving Undergraduate Education in the South.* Atlanta, Ga.: Southern Regional Education Board, 1979.

Bevan, J. M. "The Chairman: Product of Socialization or Training?" In G. French-Lazovik (Ed.), *Practices That Improve Teaching Evaluation.* New Directions for Teaching and Learning, no. 11. San Francisco: Jossey-Bass, 1982.

Hamill, P. J. *Faculty Development.* Charleston, S.C.: The College of Charleston, 1982.

Kay, S. D., and van Aalst, F. *Professional Development: A Guide for Student Affairs Staffs and Other Human Service Providers.* Charleston, S.C.: Charleston Higher Education Consortium, 1984.

Lovett, C. M., and others. "Vitality Without Mobility: The Faculty Opportunities Audit." In *Current Issues in Higher Education,* series 4. Washington, D.C.: American Association of Higher Education, 1984.

Paul J. Hamill, Jr., is assistant provost for faculty services at the College of Charleston, in South Carolina. Before becoming involved in faculty development and research administration, he served as associate registrar, focusing on student retention issues. He has also directed a college wide program for internationalizing the curriculum.

By working together, small institutions can provide major opportunities for the faculty's professional development.

Enhancing Faculty Vitality Through Collaboration Among Colleagues

Neil R. Wylie, Jon W. Fuller

A wide range of innovative and invigorating activities is possible when professors from different institutions have the opportunity to collaborate. Cooperative arrangements enable colleges and universities to pool funds and facilities as well as faculty talent in order to foster the growth and vitality of their professors. The Great Lakes Colleges Association (GLCA) has been facilitating collaborative faculty activities for more than twenty years. This case study describes the range of faculty development initiatives GLCA has supported. It also reflects on the lessons the consortium has learned from its efforts to help professors at the member colleges stay up-to-date in their fields and remain engaged in their work as college teachers.

GLCA was founded in 1961 as a multi-purpose academic consortium. Twelve institutions comprise the consortium: Albion College, Antioch University, Denison University, DePauw University, Earlham College, Hope College, Kalamazoo College, Kenyon College, Oberlin College, Ohio Wesleyan University, Wabash College, and the College of Wooster. Although they are geographically separated, they share many common institutional characteristics and values. They are small (average enrollment about fifteen hundred), residential, independent, traditional liberal arts colleges, deeply

R. G. Baldwin (Ed.). *Incentives for Faculty Vitality.* New Directions for Higher Education, no. 51. San Francisco: Jossey-Bass, September 1985.

concerned with their students' personal as well as intellectual development. Most of them are or once were church-related. They are venerable as well— most of them have recently celebrated, or are now planning, their sesquicentennials.

The need for faculty professional development opportunities at GLCA colleges can be understood by reviewing the characteristics of GLCA faculty members and the nature of their work. An overwhelming majority of GLCA faculty members earned their Ph.D.s from major graduate institutions in a traditional liberal arts discipline. Over 60 percent of the full-time GLCA faculty members are tenured. Despite their generally high level of professional qualifications, GLCA faculty members, like faculty members elsewhere, have limited mobility in today's academic marketplace.

Though this limited mobility is well known, what may be less generally understood is the work milieu in which faculty members at undergraduate liberal arts colleges operate. Although there is a stereotype of faculty members at small colleges who spend most of their time in reading and quiet reflection, occasionally lecturing brilliantly to groups of interested students, and regularly publishing thoughtful monographs and papers, the typical faculty member's experience is in reality quite different. A typical day might include teaching two classes (one introductory survey course and one for majors), tutoring a student doing an advanced undergraduate project, attending a faculty or committee meeting, counseling a student thinking about withdrawing from a course (one's own or some other), writing recommendation letters for a student applying to graduate schools, working for an hour on an article begun last summer, preparing for tomorrow's classes, and then choosing between attending a student performing arts production or a sporting event that the faculty member has been invited to by student participants.

Not all days are exactly like the one just described, but we do not believe that this description represents any significant distortion. A number of other predictable activities have been omitted, such as preparing and conducting a laboratory section or a rehearsal, reading and grading term papers, preparing examinations, registering students for courses, participating in a new-student orientation, and interviewing prospective students and their parents. A salient point emerges: The faculty members with whom we work are highly intelligent, qualified, and dedicated individuals. Their professional work environment demands of them a variety of skills for which they have received no training in graduate school (or probably anywhere else), and they have limited opportunities for participating in new professional activities or for pursuing new professional interests. Regional and national professional meetings in their disciplines do not meet all of the faculty's needs for professional training at these colleges. GLCA attempts to meet more of those needs.

Since most of the GLCA colleges enjoyed a century or more of institutional success without the benefit of consortium membership, it is perhaps surprising, but also characteristic of these institutions, that in relatively recent times they came together to form a consortium. Although no single issue or problem accounts for the founding of GLCA, it is significant that one of the earliest activities undertaken by the twelve member colleges, even before GLCA had been incorporated officially, was a conference on "Research in the Natural Sciences in Liberal Arts Colleges" (Elkin, 1982). The conference resulted in a number of recommendations for collaborative projects, including acquiring joint computer facilities, forming an affiliation with a national laboratory, exchanging science faculty and students, and collaborating with nearby universities. Not all of these suggestions were implemented. But this conference, by involving a group of GLCA faculty members directly in the process of making recommendations for the improvement of their own professional capabilities, set the example, both in style of approach and in the kind of problem to be addressed, for many of the GLCA faculty professional development activities undertaken over the years.

A general objective of GLCA is to undertake activities on behalf of its member colleges that could be better accomplished collectively than individually. One of the earliest areas of consortial success was the development of off-campus programs for GLCA students. These programs often developed following the initiative of an individual or small group of GLCA faculty members, and frequently faculty participation in the direction and management of the program was incorporated into its design. Each year, as many as nine GLCA faculty members receive a paid leave of absence to serve as director or resident faculty member for one of the GLCA off-campus programs.

A consortium is often able to assume certain kinds of programmatic risks. This has permitted GLCA to attempt programming for faculty in a number of nontraditional areas, including programmed instruction, women's studies, and most recently targeting untenured faculty as a specific professional development constituency. In addition to a willingness to try new initiatives in professional development and other areas, GLCA also has a good record of maintaining those programs that demonstrate their feasibility. To place our current professional development efforts in the larger GLCA context, our current roster of activities includes offering and promoting a dozen off-campus programs for students, exchange of management information among administrators, collective action on federal policy issues (including tax policy, financial aid, and funding for scholarly research and teaching), and a major effort in women's studies, in addition to our regular faculty professional development program.

GLCA Faculty Conferences and Workshops

After the first meeting of science faculty in 1961, a series of grants to GLCA enabled us to test a variety of approaches to faculty professional development (Elkin, 1982). The programmed instruction project just mentioned was supported in part by the U.S. Office of Education (from 1964 to 1967). This was GLCA's first attempt at promoting an innovation in instructional design, and it was only moderately successful. Another relatively early effort, supported by the Carnegie Foundation (from 1967 to 1969), attempted to provide the incentive for individual creativity and scholarship in the arts and humanities. Grants were awarded to individual faculty members to support their own artistic and scholarly work. Although a number of important projects were undertaken, it was difficult to measure significant general impact on the intellectual or esthetic life of the faculty or students at our colleges.

The initiative that did finally prove to have the greatest impact on the GLCA institutions was begun under the auspices of a grant from the Lilly Endowment (from 1975 to 1978). Appropriately, the Lilly grant proposal was written by a group of faculty members drawn together by the acting GLCA president, Laurence Barrett. As they assessed campus needs, help in improving classroom teaching was identified as the first priority.

The Lilly grant involved a mix of individual and group activities. There was funding for individual projects to promote the effectiveness of instruction and student learning. Participants were also asked to come together for summer workshops to share their new course ideas with other interested colleagues, and to explore the relationships between their personal lives and their professional lives as teachers. Shorter conferences and workshops during the academic year allowed interested colleagues to share their ideas about research and teaching. These, having proved their effectiveness, became the predominant mode of faculty professional development activities within the GLCA.

GLCA currently offers about ten faculty professional development workshops each year. They may be categorized into three different but overlapping types: conferences for people within a particular discipline, topical workshops focused on a special (often interdisciplinary) issue or problem, and workshops focused specifically on improving teaching.

In offering our conferences and workshops, we rely heavily on the expertise that already exists among GLCA faculty members. We often bring in an outsider as a "draw" for the conference or workshop, but rarely invite more than two. The most substantive and useful discussions are usually those initiated in sessions under the leadership of the GLCA faculty.

Scheduling Conferences and Workshops. Although there is no single formula guaranteed to produce a successful faculty professional development activity, certain common elements characterize our attempts in this area. Our conferences tend to be short, typically requiring only a single night's lodging away from home. We have found that the Friday–Saturday time block is acceptable to most faculty members, requiring that they miss only a single day of classes and keeping half the weekend available for personal use. Using campus locations for most of our meetings and housing participants in college inns or local motels keeps costs moderate. Selecting locations within the GLCA territory eliminates the need for air travel. Further details on the logistics of site selection, scheduling, and conference planning are available in an article by McPherson and Wylie (1983) describing a GLCA psychologists' conference.

Conference and Workshop Planning. More important than scheduling for ensuring that a workshop or conference is successful is the involvement of faculty members in the planning process. Our program is largely demand-based; that is, we provide conferences and workshops primarily addressing a specific faculty interest that has already been expressed. Although we continually seek to expand the constituencies of faculty served by our programs (sociologists and mathematicians may meet for the first time under GLCA auspices within the next year), we have found it very difficult to generate interest in a conference workshop topic that does not have the backing of at least a small core of GLCA faculty members. We use people from this core as a planning committee to generate a preliminary set of topics for the meeting, then circulate the list throughout the GLCA with a request for specific program proposals. This process ensures that our programs are never far from the current interests of our faculty. The typical division of effort between the GLCA office and the faculty core committee is to have the committee take the lead in program development and to have the office provide the logistical and administrative support.

Two GLCA faculty professional development activities that developed in this manner have now become self-sustaining. One is the annual GLCA Conference on Women's Studies. Offered in November each year since 1975, it has grown to the point where it attracts nearly two hundred participants annually—not only faculty members but also students and college administrators. More than twenty different topical sessions are offered, dealing with feminist scholarship, pedagogy, and views on society (Reed, 1982).

The other GLCA activity that is achieving permanent status is the annual Workshop on Course Design and Teaching, begun in 1977. This five-day workshop, which offers faculty members the opportunity to design or redesign courses and to examine and improve their teaching styles, is staffed primarily by a group of GLCA faculty members who have themselves gone through the course design and teaching process (Nowik, 1983). These faculty members have now taken the workshop "on the road," and have offered it at several locations in the East and Midwest.

College Support for Professional Development Efforts. The GLCA makes many efforts to achieve economy in the costs of its faculty professional development workshops. This is in part the quid pro quo for an agreement that we have with the GLCA chief academic officers to provide support for our activities. Aside from GLCA office involvement, funded by annual assessments to the member colleges, each faculty professional development activity is designed to be self-supporting. Direct conference costs, including food, lodging, and honorariums and travel for outside speakers, are assessed directly back to the college in proportion to the number of participating faculty members from their institution. The GLCA chief academic officers have been exemplary in their support of our faculty professional development efforts over the years, and see GLCA conferences and workshops as an important adjunct to programs on their individual campuses.

Campus-based faculty professional development programs typically take the form of grants for individual scholarship or course development, while GLCA activities typically involve groups of faculty members with common interests. Thus, GLCA's efforts at achieving collaboration among colleagues complement on-campus opportunities, expanding the total range of professional growth and development options available to GLCA faculty members.

Other GLCA Faculty Professional Development Options

Definition of Faculty Professional Development. What we have just described represents the core of GLCA's professional development program for faculty. However, this is only part of a much broader range of faculty opportunities. In the GLCA, we define a faculty professional development activity as any activity that provides an opportunity for a faculty member to apply existing professional competencies in a new area, to improve existing competencies, or to develop new ones. Competencies are in turn defined as those skills, knowledge, and abilities that enable a faculty member to perform effectively as a teacher, administrator, advisor, or scholar. By these definitions, a variety of other GLCA activities qualify under the general rubric of faculty professional development. Some of these will be described in the paragraphs that follow.

GLCA sponsors or co-sponsors a dozen off-campus study opportunities for students. Two of our domestic programs and four international ones require the presence of one or more of our faculty members serving for a semester or a year. Sometimes the faculty member is required to be "expert" in a particular area in order to be selected, but for our program in Japan and our European urban studies program, enthusiasm for developing a new area of scholarship may be weighted as heavily by the selection committee as the applicant's current level of expertise. Serving as a program's resident director requires the refinement and application of social and organizational skills to make the program effective. But most faculty members who lead our student off-campus programs also engage in some scholarly research, and this mix of scholarship and program leadership has typically had an important renewing effect on the participating faculty members. One recent director returned to campus to prepare a theoretical paper on the comparitive concept of the city in medieval Europe and the contemporary United States, while another returned with an interest in the relationship between early science fiction and early twentieth-century views of the Japanese people. These are both serious intellectual efforts that have been incorporated into the specific faculty member's teaching repertoire and scholarship.

Another annual GLCA activity is the New Writers Award for first published books in fiction and in poetry. Initiated and directed by a GLCA faculty member, the contest has grown until it now has more than one hundred entries submitted by publishers each year. A committee of GLCA faculty members reviews each of the works submitted. When the awards are announced, the winning authors are invited to tour the GLCA campuses, reading from their recently honored work. GLCA faculty members who take part in this program, either as the director or as reviewers, are provided an opportunity to apply their own critical and organizational skills in ways that would otherwise be only rarely available to them. They can also speak with more authority on the most recent trends in poetry and fiction.

Faculty members also have a professional development opportunity when they agree to deliver a paper at one of our conferences or read from their own works at our annual poetry festival. In addition, participation in planning and organizing our conference and workshop series provides an opportunity to exercise or develop skills in leadership and planning. Special professional status has become available for some of our faculty members who currently serve as staff members for our annual course design and teaching workshop and for those who served on the faculty of our former National Institute in Women's Studies.

GLCA regularly forms working groups to provide recommendations for GLCA policy in various areas, or to provide guidance for special projects. One such group is currently helping with the implementation of a GLCA planning grant from the Sloan Foundation, part of their program on technology and the new liberal arts. This group includes GLCA faculty members selected for their specific expertise. They will have a major role in influencing and implementing the project (the proposal for which, incidentally, was developed in consultation with another GLCA working group involving faculty members and administrators).

Prospects for the Future

Faculty professional development and renewal has become completely intertwined with the rest of GLCA's ongoing activities. This is deliberate, and reinforces our view of GLCA as an organization that takes very seriously the need of its constituent members. The direction our membership will take us in the future will depend on the needs of individual faculty members, the needs of our institutions, and changes in the higher education climate. We are only now beginning to understand some emerging themes for the near future and from the recent past. Three new areas of special concern for GLCA and its constituent colleges are now apparent.

The first area of concern is the situation of new faculty members coming into our institutions. Most of our faculty members are middle-aged, and a gap exists between their expectations about teaching, scholarship, and institutional service and the expectations of the new faculty members. New faculty members typically come to our institutions directly from graduate school or a postdoctoral research experience, and are genuinely enthusiastic about and expert in their own area of specialization. However, in almost all cases they are the only person in the institution with that specialty, and they typically find far less opportunity to pursue it than they would like. Liberal arts institutions push new faculty members to become generalists and to teach a range of introductory and other service courses within their department's curriculum. There are also pressures to serve students well through thoughtful and compassionate advising, to participate in the academic governance of the institution, and perhaps to participate in interdisciplinary courses.

To facilitate the transition of new faculty members to full professional status in our institutions and to encourage our institutions to be sensitive to issues unique to today's new faculty, with the help of a grant from the Fund for the Improvement of Postsecondary Education, we have initiated a program that focuses on new faculty matters. This program includes a series of workshops, a cross-institutional mentoring program to permit individuals with the same academic specialty but at different stages of their careers to interact, and a data base to track the careers of new faculty members coming into our institutions. This project has increased the sensitivity of many tenured faculty members and administrators to the special problems that new GLCA faculty members have in making their first major professional adjustment, and we are beginning to see reviews of institutional policies (tenure and promotion criteria, fringe benefits packages, child-care opportunities, life-style requirements) that may be having negative effects on the professional development of new faculty members.

Although GLCA has not taken a direct interest in curriculum development at our colleges since its early years, a second new area of concern suggests a cyclic trend. In conjunction with the Sloan Foundation's concerns with technology and the new liberal arts, we seek ways of assisting our liberal arts faculty members to teach new technological developments, including techniques of analysis and decision making. Our objective is, with the guidance and support of a working group from the campuses, to influence curriculum development at our colleges. The particular shape of the curricular renewal achieved will depend in large part on our experience while activities underwritten by our planning grant continue.

Finally, and least developed of these three emerging directions, is a renewed focus on minority issues in the recruitment of students and faculty and in the curriculums of our colleges. GLCA's successes in the area of women's studies, including providing support for the establishment of women's studies concentrations on several campuses, is not yet matched in the areas of minority concerns. We seek new ways of attracting minority students and faculty (the two problems are not unrelated) to our campuses. This may involve new outreach efforts to selected schools, junior colleges, and graduate programs. In this process we will undoubtedly rely on the expertise and initiative provided by a nucleus of concerned faculty members. Success in these efforts will certainly be enhanced by and will probably also lead to significant curriculum enhancements. Just as an appreciation of the new scholarship on women has led to new courses and to the revision of existing ones, so too will a renewed concern with the scholarship on and by minorities lead to similar changes. Since faculty members have direct control over the curriculum in all of our institutions, the faculty will benefit professionally both from having engaged in the change (and thus, growth) process and from gaining a sense of renewal that these curricular initiatives will bring.

Conclusion

In this chapter we have reviewed the evolution and growth of GLCA's commitment to faculty professional development, provided a sampling of the kinds of activities that we have found most effective, and suggested some directions we may take in the future. It is important to emphasize again that our program has developed in response to needs expressed by faculty members at GLCA colleges. Because they are by far the most important determiners of the directions our faculty professional development efforts will take, we take pains to keep multiple channels of communication open to faculty members. We distribute a newsletter to all GLCA faculty members several times each year, often including questionnaires and articles relating to our faculty program. We annually convene a representative faculty group, the GLCA Academic Council, to solicit their recommendations about GLCA program directions. The consortium officers regularly visit the GLCA college campuses and spend significant amounts of time in discussions with individual faculty members.

One final caution, however, is in order for those who would attempt to initiate collaborative professional development programs among faculty members from different institutions. Although our program is largely designed by and for the GLCA faculty, it could not exist without the approval and support of the key administrators at the GLCA colleges. The chief academic officers especially have been instrumental in providing this support. Through their advice and consent and through their direct financial support of faculty members from their institutions who wish to attend our programs, they play a key role in our efforts on behalf of the faculty.

One final lesson, then, is this: For a jointly sponsored faculty professional development program to be successful, it must be responsive to the needs of the faculty and involve them directly in the program development process. However, it is unlikely that any program can survive over time without the active approval and support of senior academic administrators. Balancing faculty needs and the needs perceived by chief academic officers is not as difficult as it might seem, as long as regular active channels of communication are available. But it would be a mistake to assume that any cooperative faculty professional development program could endure without devoting systematic efforts to maintaining those channels.

References

Elkin, J. L. *The Great Lakes Colleges Association: Twenty-One Years of Cooperation in Higher Education*. Ann Arbor, Mich.: Great Lakes Colleges Association, 1982.

McPherson, K. S., and Wylie, N. R. "Teaching Psychology at the Small Liberal Arts College: A Two-Day Conference." *Teaching of Psychology*, 1983, *10* (3), 144–146.

Nowik, N. "Workshop on Course Design and Teaching Styles: A Model for Faculty Development." In M. Davis, M. Fisher, S. C. Inglis, and S. Scholl (Eds.), *To Improve the Academy: Resources for Student, Faculty, and Institutional Development*. Orinda, Calif.: John F. Kennedy University, 1983.

Reed, B. "Transforming the Academy: Twelve Schools Working Together." *Change,* 1982, *14* (3), 30, 35–37.

Neil R. Wylie is vice-president of the Great Lakes Colleges Association. Previously, he served as an American Council on Education Governmental Fellow, and before that, taught psychology at Cornell College, in Mount Vernon, Iowa.

Jon W. Fuller has been president of the Great Lakes Colleges Association since 1974. During his presidency, the consortium has developed a major program emphasis on faculty professional development.

Concepts of excellence now widely adopted in business also apply to higher education.

Excellence in Business and Excellence in the Academy

Theodore J. Settle

All the nation's sectors—business, government, and education—are participating in a new movement toward excellence. The movement is signaled in business by *In Search of Excellence* (Peters and Waterman, 1982), in government by zero-deficits concepts, and in education by several major studies of excellence.

This chapter identifies a vehicle that helps organizations move toward excellence, and it explores some potential applications of excellence for presidents, chief academic officers, deans, department chairs and other academic managers involved in improving the effectiveness of the faculty resource in colleges and universities.

The Toward Excellence Program

The business community eagerly embraced the ideas and concepts in *In Search of Excellence* (Peters and Waterman, 1982). The fundamentals of excellence were clearly stated in the book and were endorsed by thousands of managers. But, because the concepts seemed difficult to implement, only a small percentage of these managers put the fundamentals into practice.

R. G. Baldwin (Ed.). *Incentives for Faculty Vitality.* New Directions for Higher Education, no. 51. San Francisco: Jossey-Bass, September 1985.

To address this problem of implementation, Zenger-Miller and Peters in 1984 developed the Toward Excellence program in Cupertino, California. In this intensive planning process, participants identify characteristics of excellence and integrate specific, detailed actions into their daily routines that are designed to accelerate progress toward excellent performance.

The process builds on five fundamental areas of competence that are common to consistently top-performing companies:

- Taking innovative action
- Getting back in touch
- Existing for the customer
- Fostering individual commitment
- Instilling unique values.

Implications for Institutions of Higher Education

The fundamentals that characterize excellence in business organizations are easily applicable to any other organization that serves clients. Action steps to foster excellence in business will also apply to other organizations. To test these hypotheses and to identify possible opportunities to develop and promote excellence, college and university administrators might ask themselves the following types of questions.

Taking Innovative Action. When was the last time you encouraged an idea from a junior faculty member? Have you ever skimmed meager resources in order to allow a faculty member to conduct research outside the traditional realm and then protected that person from other organizational requirements, such as average teaching load, filling out purchase order forms, or requesting periodic reports? Have you ever supported someone financially or psychologically primarily for their zeal and commitment rather than for a totally delineated proposal they have made?

Do senior faculty members view the nurturing and development of junior faculty members as part of their responsibility? If so, is their behavior consistent with this view? How creative is your organization? Do you take risks? Is it okay to fail? How do you reward success?

Getting Back in Touch. How often do you create a committee when you could easily talk personally with all those concerned? How much approval is required to make a trip or even a long distance telephone call? How available are you to students, faculty, and staff? When was the last time you left your office, went to a student or faculty lounge, and asked those present what was on their minds or what projects they were involved with? How often do you do this?

Do you know what department size optimizes faculty productivity? How do you encourage teamwork among faculty to maximize synergy and overall productivity? How often do you appoint a small group of faculty members to an interdisciplinary group to address a problem, explore a new area, or approach a developing opportunity? How flexible is your organizational structure?

If the collegiate experience is preparation for the remainder of one's adult life, why is so much attention concentrated on individual activity when such a high percentage of adult behavior (family, job, and personal) requires group interaction? What kind of learning environment does your faculty create? Is it the optimal environment for the students and for their circumstances in the future?

Existing for the Customer. Have you ever convened a group of your "customers" to ask them what is good and what is bad about your products? About your institution? In fact, who are your customers: students? faculty? parents? alumni? employers?

Do faculty members keep office hours, return homework promptly, have syllabuses prepared before the course begins, and alter and update their course materials as new knowledge becomes available? How much effort do they invest in making the course content interesting, exciting, and relevant? Do they teach according to their personal learning style or according to multiple learning styles? How much attention do they give to the methodology of teaching adults (which probably applies to all students) instead of the traditional, authoritarian, pedagogic style? To what extent do they view themselves as facilitators and catalysts for learning as opposed to sources of information? Overall, to what extent do faculty members listen and respond to students' educational needs to maximize the learning experience?

How do you involve business employers in your college or university? Are they primarily viewed as sources of funds for your programs or projects? Do you solicit their opinions on your curriculums, policies, and quality of graduates? Do you choose to operate independently from employers, or does your behavior exhibit a conviction that the entire society benefits from greater partnerships between the important sectors of education and employers? Is it to your advantage to be independent of or interdependent with employers?

Does your college or university have an executive with "quality" in his or her title? If so, does this person report to the president or chief executive officer as a means of emphasizing the importance of the function to the entire organization? How many presidents, chief academic officers, deans, and department chairs have student, staff, or faculty committees whose sole function is to improve quality in the organization? How high a priority is this on your campus?

Fostering Individual Commitment. Does your institution offer supervisory or management training when a faculty member becomes the department chair or when a department chair becomes a dean? Does your institution offer how-to-teach and proposal-writing courses for faculty members and graduate assistants, communications skills for all employees, and team-building for faculty and administrative support personnel within the same department?

As the information explosion continues and solutions to problems require more interdisciplinary efforts, how do you encourage the development of and synergy from effective work teams across departments rather than from a collection of individuals within a department? Why do colleges and universities, organizations with significant continuing education requirements to keep faculty members current in their disciplines, place such an apparently low priority on internal staff development in the professional and managerial skills that are necessary for long-term success?

Instilling Unique Values. At present, what makes your organization special? What differentiates your college or university from another institution down the road? What does your institution do especially well? What is your market niche? In the future, what kind of place do you want your college or university to be?

For how long can you sacrifice efficiency in organization, optimal motivation, and maximum productivity due to the absence of an institutional rallying point? Can you ignore the recent enrollment success of many narrowly focused institutions? Keeping in mind your institution's needs, first for immediate survival and second, for longevity and vitality, can your institution afford to lack clarity of purpose?

Are you willing to commit yourself to identifying a mission and act as a leader for the university community? Are you willing to invest the effort to gain the synergy that results from a narrowed sense of purpose combined with broad-based support?

The movement toward excellence is a process of envisioning the future and then developing and implementing the actions that are necessary to achieve excellence. The future, although dimly seen, is ours to influence. The attitudes and values we hold and the ways we do our everyday tasks can add up to excellence—the necessary ingredient to long-term organizational success.

Reference

Peters, T. J., and Waterman, R. H. *In Search of Excellence: Lessons from America's Best-Run Companies.* New York: Harper & Row, 1982.

Theodore J. Settle is the director, NCR Management College at NCR Corporation in Dayton, Ohio. Previously, he had nine years' experience in higher education at Tuskegee Institute, in Alabama; the University of Michigan; and the Illinois Board of Higher Education.

The editor offers closing comments.

Concluding Comments

Roger G. Baldwin

Vitality takes many forms in the academic profession. The chapters in this volume have demonstrated that numerous types of encouragement and support are necessary to sustain the energy and productivity of professors who possess a wide range of interests and capabilities and who work in diverse institutional settings. Hamill's colorful metaphor succinctly summarizes the principal message of this source book. We need an extensive "arsenal" of incentives to enhance the vitality of college and university professors.

We have learned from the preceding chapters, however, that creating a climate conducive to faculty vitality requires more than an assortment of rewards and reinforcements. Proper use of incentives requires sensitivity and precision—the skill of a surgeon and the creativity of an artist. Incentives applied without recognition of individual needs or institutional realities will fail to elicit the slightest spark of vigor from faculty members. Carefully managed incentives, in contrast, can release the energy and resourcefulness of the talented men and women who staff higher education institutions.

Fortunately, colleges and universities have an extensive array of incentives on which to draw. Bowen reminds us that tangible incentives, such as merit pay, research grants, funds to purchase equipment, and library holdings, can enhance faculty morale and performance. Less tangible or less direct incentives, such as faculty forums, recognition in campus publications, and a stimulating colleague climate, can also motive professors to

R. G. Baldwin (Ed.). *Incentives for Faculty Vitality.* New Directions for
Higher Education, no. 51. San Francisco: Jossey-Bass, September 1985.

achieve their potential productivity. Schuster discusses the incentive value of a work environment that provides the tools of research and means for intellectual refreshment while protecting professors from excessive demands that easily deplete their creative energies.

The authors especially urge colleges and universities to capitalize on incentives that motivate faculty behavior naturally. Hamill asserts that such catalytic extrinsic incentives as small grants actually provide outlets for the professions inherent incentives, as for example, autonomy, love of learning, fellowship, and concern for student development. Lawrence suggests that the developmental drive for meaningful work as well as the desire to guide the direction of one's career present powerful forces that, with close communication, can be harnessed for the benefit of the individual and the institution. Wylie and Fuller show how opportunities to learn and collaborate with colleagues can be an energizing experience for professors. Conditions that enable professors to pursue the activities that first attracted them to the academic profession can help to unleash ambitions that often lie dormant but remain alive in the academic's psyche.

Bevan argues that a flexible definition of academic responsibilities can act as an incentive for faculty members. Viewing the faculty broadly as educational resources rather than as narrow knowledge specialists gives professors more avenues for intellectual excitement. It can encourage professors to interact, exchange ideas from their various fields, contribute to one another's classes, and collaborate on research. Like other authors, Bevan asserts that academic institutions must provide a structure that reinforces community and enhances professors' power to carry out their duties creatively and effectively. To achieve this end, persons in authority who control resources and regulate schedules and work loads must be must be willing to adjust academic procedures to deliver effective incentives when and where they are needed.

Incentives to enhance faculty vitality present many logistical problems that require thoughtful solutions. Hamill describes the institutional acrobatics necessary to make available the resources, time, and moral support needed to foster the professional activity of academics from different fields and career stages. Wylie and Fuller make clear that careful planning with heavy faculty involvement is required to implement cooperative professional development programs that genuinely meet faculty needs. Each chapter offers evidence that incentives are effective as part of a stimulating and supportive environment. Without careful coordination of work load arrangements, rewards systems, and other personnel policies, the effectiveness of any one incentive is likely to be minimal.

The authors' examples of effective incentives, however, are illustrative rather than comprehensive. The common objective of the writers is to encourage professors and academic administrators to think creatively about the types of incentives that will most effectively promote high-quality work by faculty members. Baldwin and Krotseng's analysis of the incentives employed successfully in selected high-performance corporations should help to expand our thinking beyond the sometimes impenetrable boundary that separates the academic world from other complex "people organizations."

Although the various chapters recommend many different strategies to foster faculty vitality, some degree of consensus appears to emerge concerning the basic nature and application of effective faculty incentives. The authors agree that incentives must be employed flexibly. Incentives that respond to individual differences and organizational conditions will be more effective than those that try to invigorate all faculty members by the same methods.

There is also considerable agreement on the important role of academic leadership in employing incentives. Leaders can release creative faculty efforts by clarifying institutional goals and by channeling professors' energy through the careful management of opportunity, support, and recognition.

Finally, a sense emerges from the various chapters that effective incentives enable professors to capitalize on the best that academic life has to offer, to pursue the challenges and reap the satisfactions inherent in an academic career. Opportunities to follow new interests, to assume new assignments, and to grow professionally seem more likely to provoke dynamic faculty activity than does the possibility of a salary increase or promotion to a higher rank.

A climate conducive to faculty vitality is comprised of a host of diverse, flexible, and well-coordinated incentives. Schuster's mathematical model helps us to think about the sources of vitality in concrete and specific terms. This volume has identified the main elements of a stimulating academic environment—lively, intellectually acute faculty; challenging students; a supportive and goal-oriented administration; flexible personnel policies; and adequate resources. Each unique higher education institution, however, must combine these components in the proper proportions to maintain creative ferment among its faculty members. Because academic lives are dynamic and institutional histories evolve, colleges and universities must continually fine tune their incentive systems. There is no simple or final answer to the question: What incentives are needed to enhance faculty vitality?

Toombs' analysis of broad contextual factors related to faculty vitality necessarily raises the discussion of incentives from the individual level to the collective level. He sees current circumstances within higher education institutions, the disciplines, and the academic profession working against the vitality of the professoriate. Toombs suggests that incentives aimed solely at the individual faculty member will not be adequate to sustain the vigor and productivity of the profession as a whole. Incentives that promote narrow, special purpose scholarship and faculty competition must be balanced by incentives that favor cooperation, collegiality, and a collective identity for the professoriate. Academic organizations and policies that enlist professors in a common professional cause greater than their individual intellectual activities should enhance the well-being of faculty members in general.

Higher education's increased awareness of the issue of faculty vitality and the complex conditions that support it is a move in the right direction. Greater concern for faculty vitality will help colleges and universities to develop the policies and provide the support necessary to maintain energetic, up-to-date faculty members.

The goal of a higher education institution is to create a climate that stimulates all of its faculty members—not just its stars—and rewards their contributions to the educational program. Incentives must foster the many forms of excellence necessary to sustain high-quality education in an era of rapid change.

The faculty vitality equation outlined in this volume should aid colleges and universities in assessing the various incentives and the overall work environment they offer to professors. The equation, although rough, should help academic leaders and faculty committees to define incentive strategies that can invigorate the diverse faculty on their campuses.

However, Toombs makes it clear that the vitality issue cannot be addressed fully at the departmental or institutional level. State higher education systems, disciplinary associations, and national umbrella higher education organizations must also cooperate to develop an environment that sustains a vigorous academic profession.

Settle's chapter on "excellence" reminds us that higher education is not alone in its quest for conditions that promote vitality. More importantly, perhaps, he urges us on to action. He suggests that we think imaginatively, experiment, and try multiple approaches. Most of all, he encourages us to begin. This is appropriate advice at the conclusion of a book concerned with faculty vitality. We will never achieve our objective if we do not take some risks and get started.

Roger G. Baldwin is assistant professor of higher education at the College of William and Mary, in Williamsburg, Virginia.

Index

117

118

Department chair: incentive building by, 48–50; and incentives management, 89

DePauw University, collaboration by, 99–100

Developmental needs: analysis of, 59–68; background on, 59–60; conclusion on, 66; for control of environment, 60–61, 63, 64–65; and incentives, 15–16, 59–68; for meaning of work, 61–62, 63; and person-environment fit, 62–66; themes in, 60–62

Disciplines: and faculty vitality, 73–76, 80; future trends in, 74–75

Douvan, E., 61, 68

Dry, J., 67

E

Earlham College, collaboration by, 99–100

Elkin, J. L., 101, 102, 108

Ely, R. T., 72

Erikson, E. H., 60, 61, 67

Excellence: in business and in the academy, 109–112; fundamentals for, 110–112; program for, 109–110

Exxon, 92

F

Faculty: academic role of, 62–63; compensation for, 12–13, 25; concerns of, 62–64; and control of environment, 60–61, 63, 64–65; developmental needs of, 15–16, 59–68; faculty vitality viewed by, 21–32; and meaning of work, 61–62, 63; mid- to late-career stage of, 65–66; new members of, 106; pre-retirement stage of, 66; pre-tenure stage of, 64–65; professional context of, 69–82; as resource pool, 47–48; "speed-up" for, 6–7; tenure to mid-career stage of, 65; visiting, 42–43, 47; work milieu of, 9–10, 100; work week of, 34; workshops for, 40–41, 101–104

Faculty development: analysis of collaboration for, 99–108; background on, 99–101; concept of, 104; conclusion on, 107–108; conferences and workshops for: 40–41, 101–104; director of: incentives building by,

52–53; established, as incentive, 84–86; and faculty vitality, 29; future for, 105–107; options for, 104–105; practices for, 78–79

Faculty forum, as incentive, 30, 41–42

Faculty vitality: and academic freedom, 27; administrative leadership for, 26, 30, 31–32; characteristics of, 56; and collaboration with colleagues, 27, 99–108; and compensation, 12–13, 25; concepts of, 1, 7, 23, 70; conclusions on, 113–116; conditions affecting, 7–10; context for study of, 22–23; correlates of, 23–27; and course variations, 29–30; creative leaves for, 30; and disciplines, 73–76, 80; environment for, 10; extrinsic factors in, 8; facilitating of, 53–54; faculty forums for, 30, 41–42; faculty view of, 21–32; formula for, 10–11, 28; hiring for, 30–31; importance of, 1; and incentives, 5–20; inhibiting of, 55–56; and institutions, 76–80; intangible factors in, 25–26; and intellectual refreshment, 24, 30; intrinsic factors in, 7–8; lessons on, 28–29; and profession of academic work: 70–73, 80; professional context for, 69–82; and research tools, 23–24; and sense of community, 26–27; strategies for, 29–31; and students, 24–25; tangible factors in, 23–25; and work conditions, 9–10, 100; and work load, 25, 30; and work load contracts, 30

Finkelstein, M. J., 9, 19, *21,* 70, 73, 82

Finn, C. E., 5–6, 19

Fitzpatrick, W., 62, 68

Flexner, A., 73, 82

Foster, P. J., *21*

Fowler, D., 67

Franklin and Marshall College, Center for Faculty Exchange at, 43

French-Lazovik, G., 89

Frye, B. E., 6, 19

Fuller, J. W., 3, 99–108, 114

Fund for the Improvement of Postsecondary Education, 91, 106

G

Gamson, Z. T., 6–7, 8, 18

Gardner, J. W., 7, 19

German, K., 63, 67

Shils, E., 72–73, 82
Sloan Foundation, 105, 106
Smith, D. K., 6, 19
Smith, H. E., 53, 57
Smutz, W. D., 71, 82
Sommer, S., 92
Spector, B., 18
Stanford University, and academic freedom, 72
Strauss, A., 70, 81
Students, and faculty vitality, 24–25
Sumner, W. G., 72

T

Teachers Insurance Annuity Association—College Retirement Equity Fund, 72, 82
Temple University, and professional behavior, 72
Texas Instruments, 14
Thomas, M. W., 70, 82
Toombs, W., 2, 69–82, 115–116
Touraine, A., 80, 82
Trinity University, and League of Institutions for Faculty Exchange (LIFE), 42
TRW, 12, 13
Tuckman, H. P., 8, 15, 16, 19
Tupperware, 13

U

Unions, and faculty vitality, 29
U.S. Office of Education, 92, 102
Uwalaka, O. A., 77–79, 82

V

van Aalst, F., 91, 97
Veblen, T., 69, 82
Veroff, J., 61, 68
Veysey, L. R., 7–8, 9, 19
Vitality. See Faculty vitality
Vollmer, M. M., 70, 82

W

Wabash College, collaboration by, 99–100
Waldman, D. A., 13, 19
Walton, R. E., 18
Waterman, R. H., Jr., 11, 12, 13, 14, 19, 63, 68, 109, 112
Western Electric, 12
White, F., 62, 68
William and Mary, College of, incentives at, 37, 40, 42
Wisconsin University of, and academic freedom, 72
Wise, W. M., 46, 57
Wooster, College of, collaboration by, 99–100
Workshops. See Conferences and workshops
Wylie N. R., 3, 99–108, 114

Y

Yale University and academic freedom, 72

Z

Zenger-Miller program, 110
Znaniecki, F., 70, 82